Connection

CCY ARCHITECTS

Foreword by Rick Sommerfeld

Contents

Foreword

By Rick Sommerfeld

The landscape of the American West is a diverse and powerful phenomenon that is both undeniable and formidable. As architects integrate buildings into the natural beauty of these settings, a sensitivity to the history of the place, the materiality of the land, and the integration into the climate is a prerequisite. For more than forty years, CCY Architects has been working to establish meaningful connections to the places and the clients they serve.

The projects in this monograph showcase CCY's polyvalent approach to design. Each architectural solution layers function, form, and varying facets of the building's location into tacit experiences. Their meticulous detailing shows the care taken in articulating the poetry of form; the craftsmanship of CCY projects speaks to the valuable relationships they have built with contractors who help bring the buildings to life.

Their reverence for place begins in the earliest stages of the design process. CCY's practice of site visits—so intensive that they are thought of as interviews—leverages both the opportunities and constraints of a distinct location to derive their architectural language. The slight undulation of a meadow, wind patterns, restrictive building requirements, steep topography, or even the liabilities of building near a debris field help guide each project's experience. Approach, procession, and arrival are highly curated. The residences appear quiet and humble in the land, but the interiors are spacious and filled with light. Expansive views of distant mountains are balanced with purposefully intimate moments, creating pause and allowing the setting to be experienced in new ways. This methodology roots the project in its landscape and establishes a constant dialogue with the surroundings.

The clients' characteristics are imbued in each project, an assimilation of how they live, work, and recreate. It is clear that CCY's design process is a collaborative one. Great attention is paid to how the public and private programs are arranged. Through the articulation of these relationships, both interior and exterior spaces artfully unfold in response to the individual project criteria.

CCY's fundamental understanding of material reinforces these spatial sequences. Concrete, stone, wood, glass, and steel are deftly manipulated to resonate with the building's occupants and detailed to create profound connections to the architectural ideas. Material palettes evoke the natural surroundings, and sunlight animates rooms with shadow play. Windows open to the smell of sage and colors recall the bark of the trees set against the white of snow. Spaces are brought alive by the skillful application of materials and textures. CCY designs environments. They are atmospheric, nuanced, tactile, and haptic.

Juhani Pallasmaa, the noted Finnish architect and scholar, argues that "one of the grave mistakes in today's architectural thinking is the separation of aesthetics as an autonomous category." The work of CCY shows us the importance of connecting aesthetics to a region and to individual clients. This integration allows the buildings to enhance the way we live and gives us a greater appreciation for the authenticity of place.

Introduction

This book is a conversation about design and the land. The houses inside these pages and the essays "Uncovering" and "Connecting" illustrate an approach, evolved over our many collective years of working and living in places of natural beauty, that embraces a derivation of modern architecture that is integral to its environment and honestly celebrates its connection to the land.

Our process begins with interviewing each site to uncover attributes which inform a more meaningful architecture and an optimal dialogue between the two, an exercise equal parts digging deep and attentive listening, with the process actively informing the finished work. This ethos reflects both our intention to create highly sophisticated designs, and who we are as a team: approachable, down-to-earth, and appreciative of our environment and community.

We live and practice in the Roaring Fork Valley of Colorado, home to the intellectual and artistic community of Aspen. Drawn to the community's focus on the pursuit of mind, body, and spirit and the integration of the experience of nature, we strive to find architectural solutions reflective of that equilibrium; we place a high value on the irreplaceable physicality of each site, the visions of each client, and the combination of those to create the spirit of each place. The rigorous pursuit of design in a retreat-like natural setting encourages, for us, an invigorating and inspiring exploration of an alternative expression of contemporary architecture.

In addition to our residential work, our practice includes hotels, new communities, and one-of-a-kind commissions in places as scattered as New England, the Mongolian foothills, the California desert, and the Caribbean islands. Regardless of project or location, the process of uncovering and connecting is a constant. Sharpened by different ecologies and cultures, it is the foundation for architecture that creates more connection to place and, through that, a richer human experience.

Castle Creek

05 03

Castle Creek Valley, Colorado
19 Acres
Blue Zone
Forces of Nature
Picturesque
Upper Meadow
The Pond
Unfolding
Hayden Peak
Roof That Flies
Articulated Spine
Light Shelf
Editing

04 27

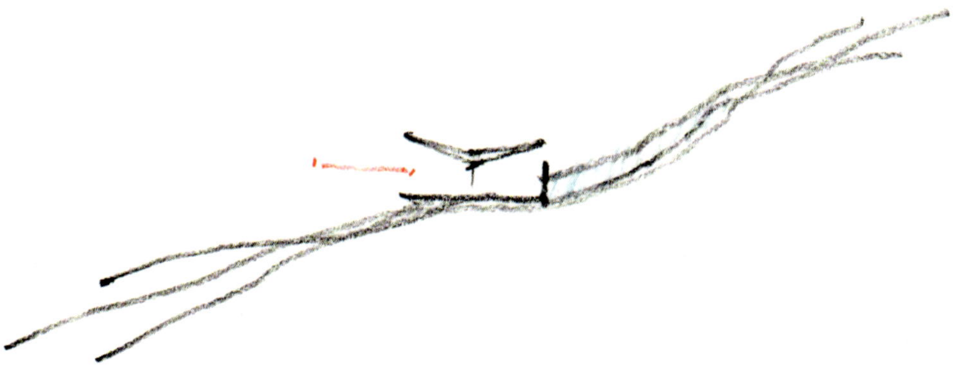

THE LIGHT OF VENICE

The homesite sits in an alpine meadow bounded by an aspen forest and slopes down to long-distance views. The owners asked for a sophisticated home on a single level that would engage the meadow and allow them to enjoy indoor-outdoor living and entertaining. Because summer, with its invitation to live outdoors, is short-lived at 8,500 feet in elevation, it became important to identify ways to connect the house to the land at other times of the year.

The prescribed building envelope contains a minor avalanche path. Inspiration for the home's butterfly roof came from the uphill-downhill nature of the site and the dichotomy it presented: from above, it required protection from potential avalanches and, from below, openness to the sun-filled, expansive views. On the uphill side, thick structural walls provide avalanche protection while large window walls on the downhill side work with the butterfly to visually expand space to terraces and views beyond.

To maintain one-story living, the plan is articulated in separate pavilions that follow the curving topography. Each pod is defined by a separate roof section. The corners open to high ridgelines and to light filtered through an aspen grove, connecting the interiors to the forest and ridges as they change with the seasons.

The design incorporates fundamentals of passive solar design: the building opens to the south, is minimally exposed to the north, and tucks into the hillside. Optimal roof overhangs admit winter sun while minimizing summer heat gain, and the light shelves reflect daylight deep into the interior.

In recognition of the avalanche path, the thickness of the avalanche wall is expressed in the window openings on the interior, hinting at the work it might be asked to do. Its massiveness contrasts with the slender steel columns, stacking window walls, and shallow light shelf of the southern walls. Throughout the interior, a steel band announces the juncture of the two roof planes; walls purposefully cross the juncture, emphasizing the geometry.

The house is open and flowing in the summer months, with ample terraces for mornings and evenings outdoors. In the winter, it feels like a refuge tucked into the hillside, revealing unexpected glimpses of nature all around.

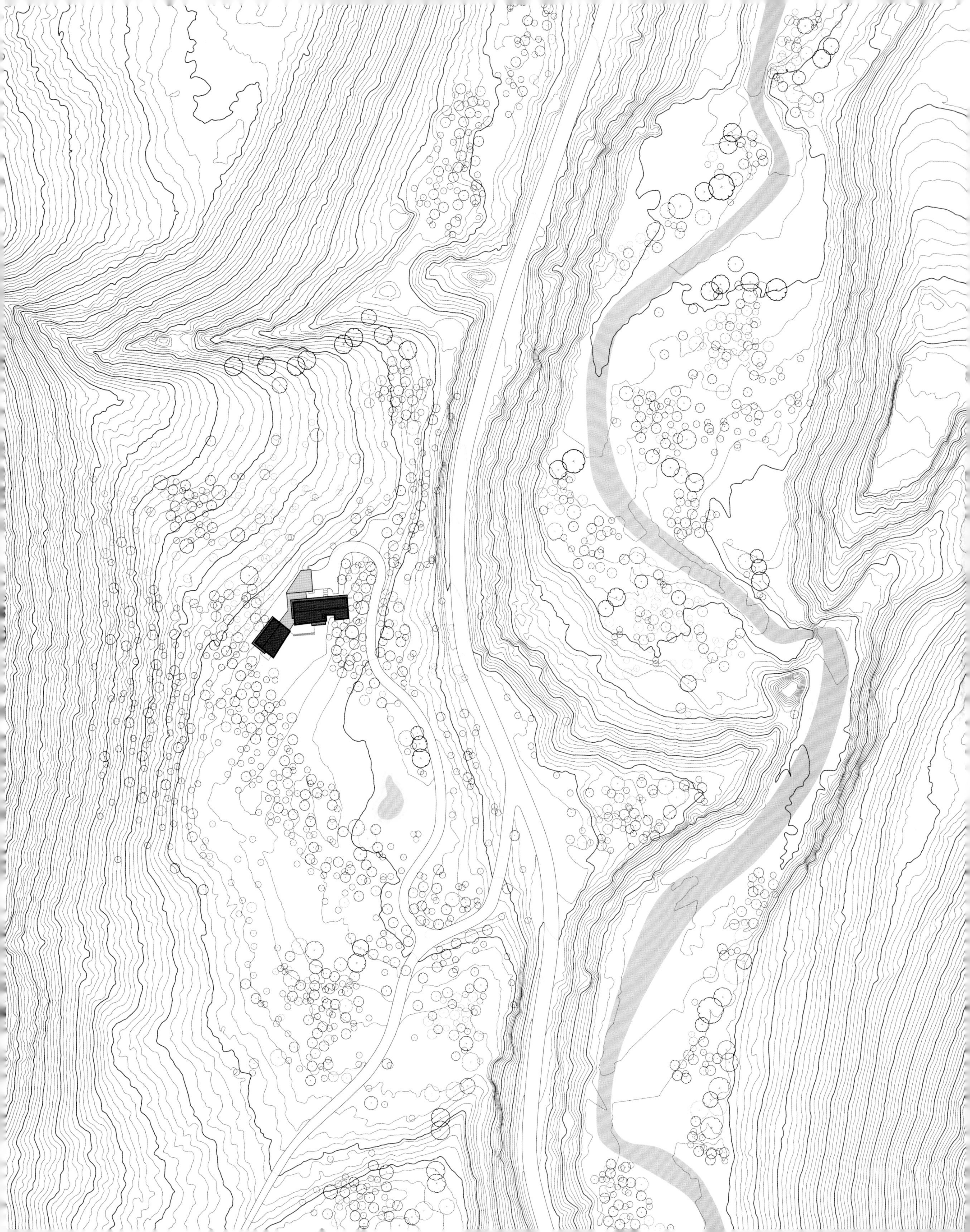

Opposite: A window in the thick wall of the primary bath opens to the forest.

Top right: The restrained palette of honed sandstone and stained oak in the kitchen reflects the edited palette throughout the house.

Bottom right: A corner of the den opens to engage the aspen forest.

Victorian Music Box

10 14

West End, Aspen
The Ellen Kelley House
1888, 1970, 2018
Paper Stacks
Music, Art and Classical Forms
Porosity of Site
Axial Spaces
Deference
Acoustical
Dot Mockups
Nocturne in E-Flat Major, Op. 9, No. 2
Day to Night, Inside and Out

08 24

229

Aspen's West End neighborhood is an inspired mix of restored historic structures, creative new ones, and a campus that caters to cultural and intellectual pursuits, including the Benedict Music Tent and Aspen Center for Physics. A couple purchased an 1880s Victorian in the West End because of its proximity to the Music Tent and their affinity for historical architecture. The couple wanted the Victorian's small spaces to live larger and have a stronger connection to the outdoors. The design reflects their interests in architecture and the arts and the wife's particular passion for classical piano.

The resulting compound marries the restored Victorian with a modern, music-inspired guesthouse, affectionately called the Music Box, designed to accommodate guests as well as music recitals.

The form and scale of the Music Box are respectful of the architectural heritage around it, but the material attitude contrasts with the ornamented Victorian. A single material—aluminum—bent with four-inch exposures, covers the roof and walls.

Capturing daylight in the Music Box posed a challenge that was met by perforating the siding. This filtered out unwanted alley views and also harsh western light. The design for the perforations was created in a pattern derived from Chopin's Nocturne in E-Flat Major, Op. 9, No. 2, a favorite composition of the wife's, superimposed on the building elevations like sheet music. The dappled light that fills the Music Box is brought deeper into the space by continuous perforations in the stair.

The Music Box's small living area is spatially static but dynamic in experience, as the ever-changing light patterns move through the space. For acoustic attenuation, oak woodwork is striated with saw cuts, creating a corduroy-like texture. The Victorian contrasts with the Music Box both spatially and materially. To make spaces in the Victorian feel larger, its tight rooms are linked with calm axial connections that open up the interior and blend into the terrace, allowing both indoor and outdoor spaces to feel larger. Interior detailing is muted and sophisticated, fitting for this house and complying with the atmosphere the owners wished to create.

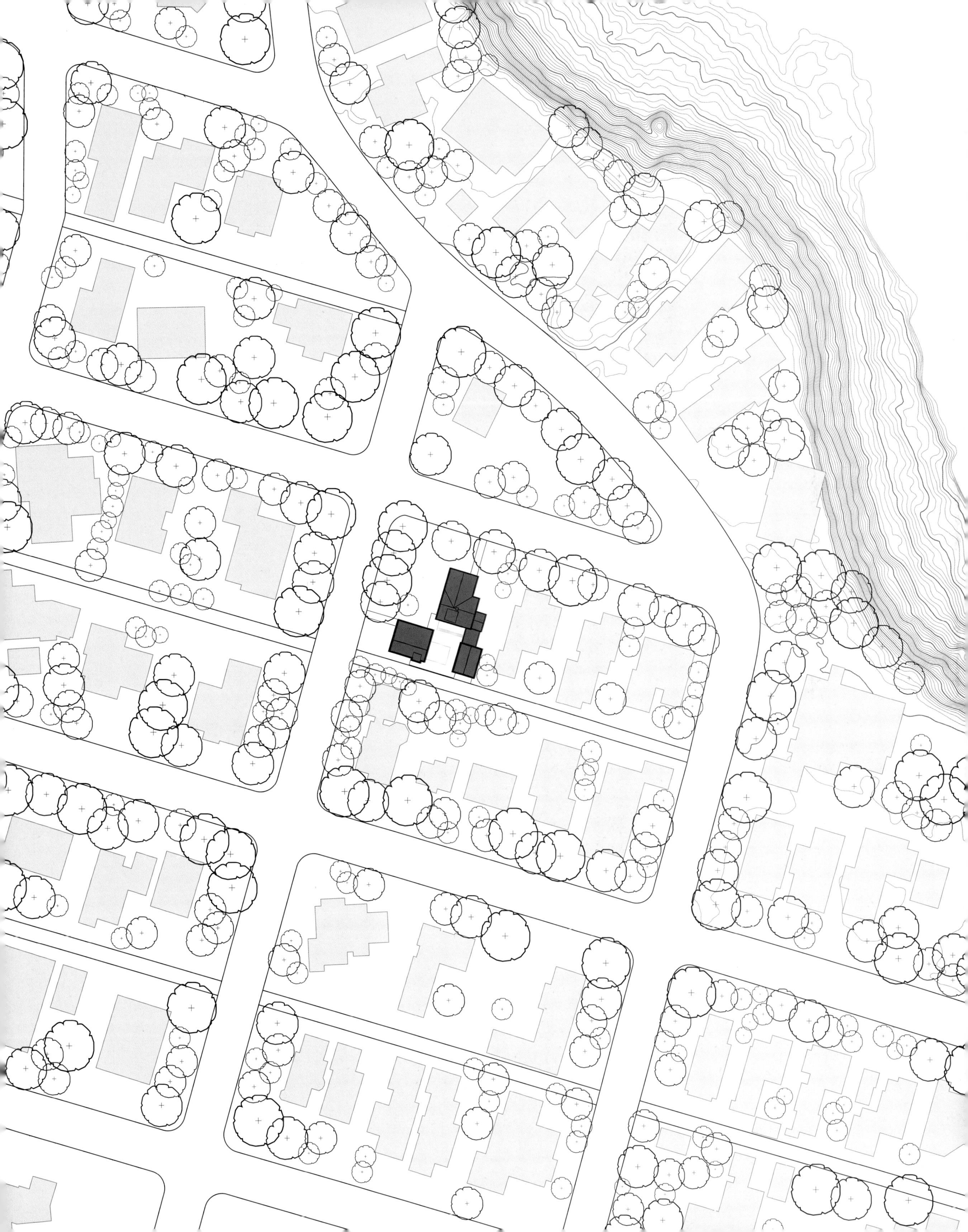

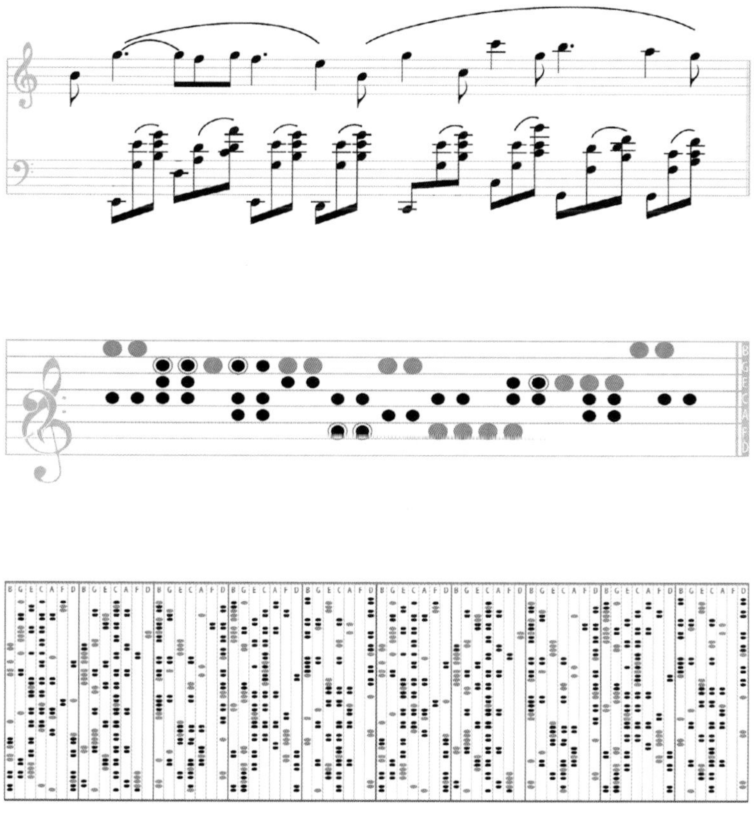

Top left: To create the facade from a piece of music, the distinct chords and notes from Chopin's Nocturne in E-Flat Major, Op. 9, No. 2 (top) were assigned a hole or pattern size (middle), with hole size corresponding to pitch and number of holes to the duration of the note (bottom).

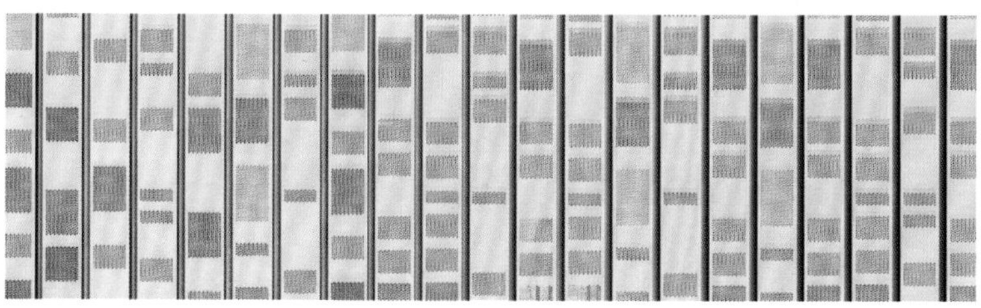

Bottom left: Each piece of the aluminum siding's laser-cut patterns is unique, representing different parts of the musical score.

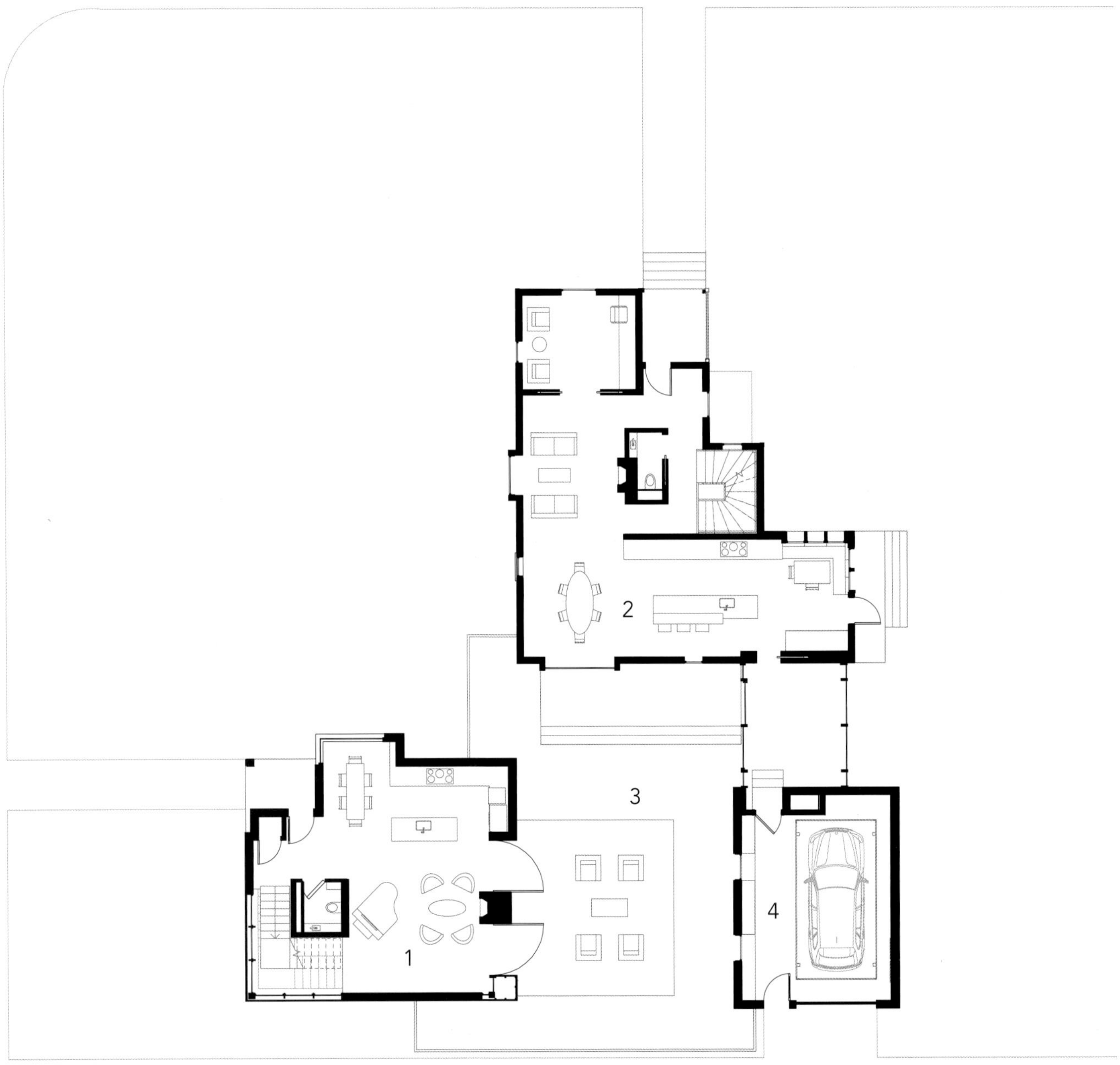

1 - Music Box
2 - Victorian
3 - Courtyard
4 - Garage

Top left: Opening up axial connections in the Victorian creates longer sight lines to better appreciate the home's calm, muted palette, as shown here in the entry to the living room.

Bottom left: An original window in the dining area preserves historic character while embracing the modern interior.

T.A.G.

10 12

Pitkin County, Colorado
4.4 Acres
Two Generations
Aspen Grove
Winding Approach
Views and Sun
Solitude
Precedent Gable
Substance and Stone
Cool Spectrum
Inspired Choices
Evolving Constant
What Does It Stand For?

12 01

This family compound creates a gathering place that defines and embraces the lifestyles of multiple generations. The parents reside in the main house and the next generation lives part-time in the guesthouse. A progressive approach to traditional architecture sets the stage for different attitudes to play out in the interior spaces.

The clients desired a home which was generally traditional, while the next generation preferred a more contemporary orientation. The exterior forms and materials needed to bridge the gap and accommodate both attitudes. To achieve this, classic gable roofs, which have signified home for centuries, serve as the identifying form of the compound, but are rendered in crisp detail. Stone, another timeless material, is used in elemental, abstracted ways.

In the main house, large window walls in the public realms capture expansive views and sun, while private spaces look out onto stands of nearby aspens. The exterior palette makes its way inside where there is a strong stone presence and muted grey tones that key off the stone. Spaces link in comfortable sequences.

The guesthouse creates its own environment; spaces are tighter and more inward-looking. Exterior materials and colors are discarded on the inside and replaced with a lighter palette including whitewashed wood, white lacquered cabinets, and Carrara marble. Of necessity in the smaller house, elements and spaces are multifunctioning. On the lower level, a wet room efficiently contains the tub, shower and vanity. Next to it, a subgrade dressing room and walk-in closet are adjacent to a translucent wall that brings daylight into the space and creates a shadow play of those walking the stairs.

As the compound ages, the bright copper will patina to a rich dark brown in the Rocky Mountain climate. As it visually recedes, the stone will appear more prominent, changing the perception of the exterior and subtly symbolizing this legacy property.

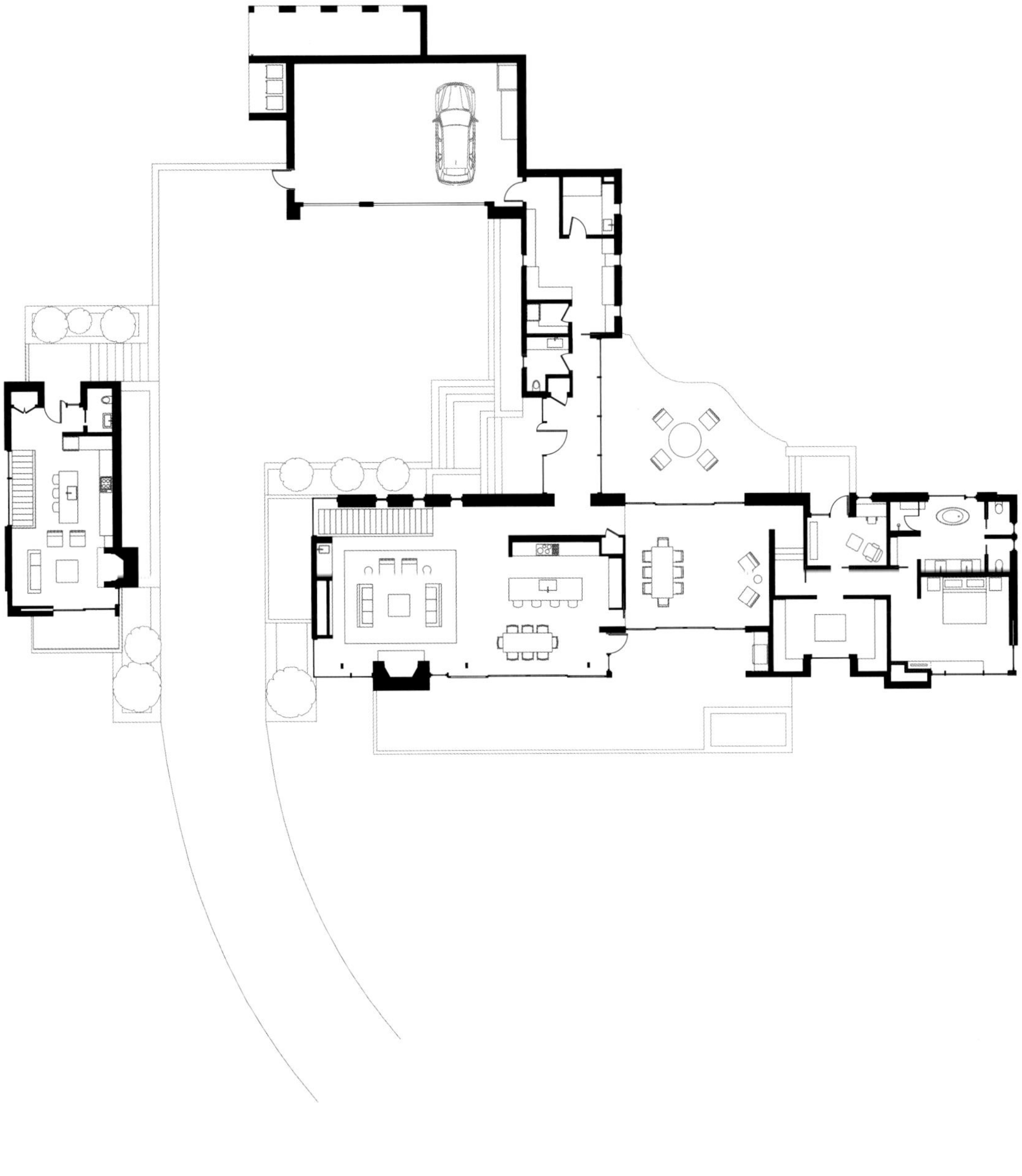

Previous spread: Exterior stone and cedar siding have a strong presence inside the main house. A terminus wall and art signal entry to the primary suite.

Above: The entry is an interlocking composition of stained cedar, stone, and art.

Left: The kitchen elegantly recedes into the space. Mocha-stained oak anticipates the future tone of copper used on the exterior in another inside-out connection.

White walls, bleached oak, and Carrara marble create a contemporary palette in the guesthouse. A board-formed concrete fireplace provides textural contrast.

Next spread: Translucent glass at the stairway brings light and a little magic into the lower-level dressing area.

Gambel Oaks

09 23

Missouri Heights, Colorado
43 + 161 Acres
Finding Place
Conservation Easement
Meandering Arrival
6 Pink Gates
The Pasture
Low on the Land
Western Saddle
Local Artisans
Earthy and Eclectic
30 Chickens, 10 Horses
8 Goats, 3 Cats, 2 Dogs
Community Serving
D.W.T.F.Y.W. Ranch

11 17

The owner defined precise requirements for her home: it should reflect her love of nature and progressive attitude toward resource conservation, be invisible from any nearby roads, and achieve LEED Gold Certification from the US Green Building Council.

From the entry drive approach, the house is revealed in a series of glimpses, culminating at a courtyard that constrains the expansive landscape. A trio of corten steel boxes, approximating the spacing and scale of the site's Gambel oaks that grow savanna-like in interspersed groves, both organize the compound and create a subtle tie to the land. The primary roof, which spans the two masses containing the living spaces, lifts quietly above the steel and allows space to flow outdoors. Sight lines build seamlessly from interior spaces to outdoor terraces, a lap pool, and to pastures, lake, and mountains beyond.

Exterior spaces invite a variety of experiences. The lap pool is tucked low in the ground with minimal terracing, emphasizing immersion in nature. A second-story deck is a promontory over the expansive landscape, and an exterior shower becomes a private retreat where architecture and nature intertwine.

The materials work to achieve related goals. The gabion walls, built with the help of the owner from site-collected stone, and the rusted steel boxes connect the structure to the land, while locally sourced stone and beetle kill pine contributed to the home attaining LEED Gold Certification.

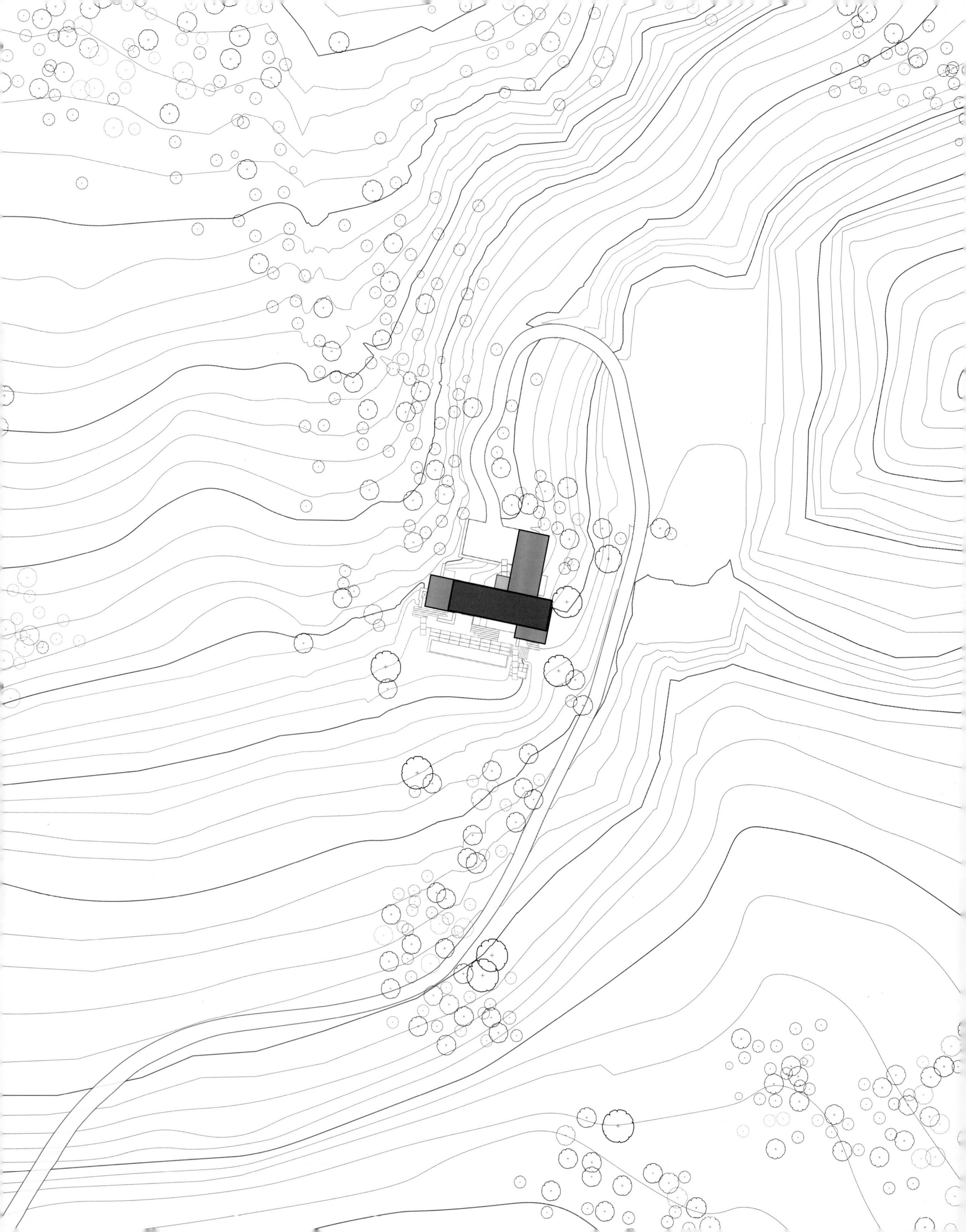

Opposite: A yoga studio, flowing seamlessly onto a terrace, is the only space perched above the meadow on the second level, providing a different relationship to the landscape.

Right: Gabion walls and corten steel are composed to create a private outdoor shower.

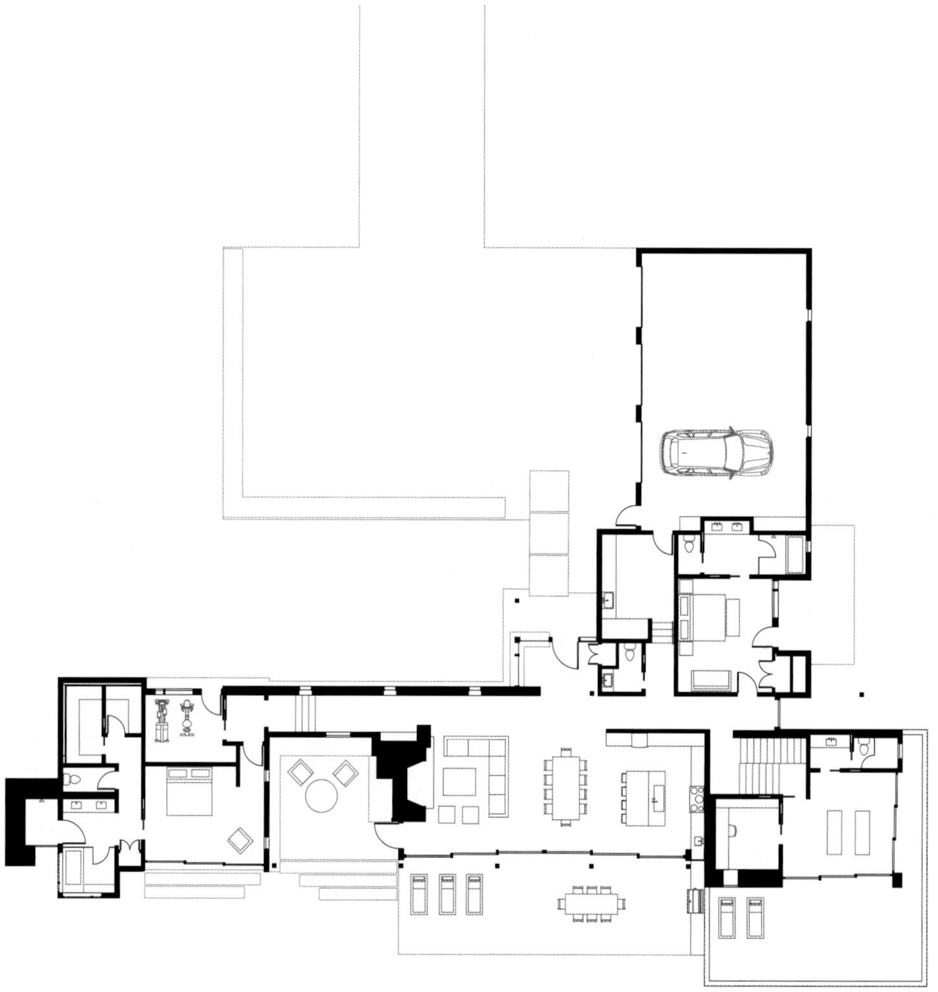

Opposite: The living room fireplace has a gabion figure set into a larger field of grey sandstone. The two stones are a distillation of the landscape—the grey sandstone echoes tones in the surrounding mountains and the gabion stones are collected from the site.

Above: Tucked around the corner, the outdoor room fireplace repeats the compositional ideas.

The primary bedroom opens directly onto the meadow, cocooned within a gradually layered space from the beetle kill pine bed nook to exterior corten walls.

Uncovering

We're here to interview the land,
to understand its challenges
and opportunities.

The powerful natural landscapes of the West have been formative to our thought process. If we think of architecture as something that exists within an environment, like an organism, then our approach can be described as an ecology of place, where architecture is integrally linked to site-specific factors. And if we observe both the dynamic and static relationships within an environment, we can uncover layers of information which define a value system unique to each site and client.

We fasten our snowshoes at 10,250 feet above sea level. It's a February afternoon in the Colorado Rockies and the temperature might reach above freezing for only a few hours before the sun dips behind the ridge. Twenty-mile-an-hour winds are predicted, and thick white clouds form over the peaks. Blankets of snow absorb sound; when the wind calms, our footsteps cut sharply through the silence. We're here to interview the land, to understand the challenges and opportunities of this place.

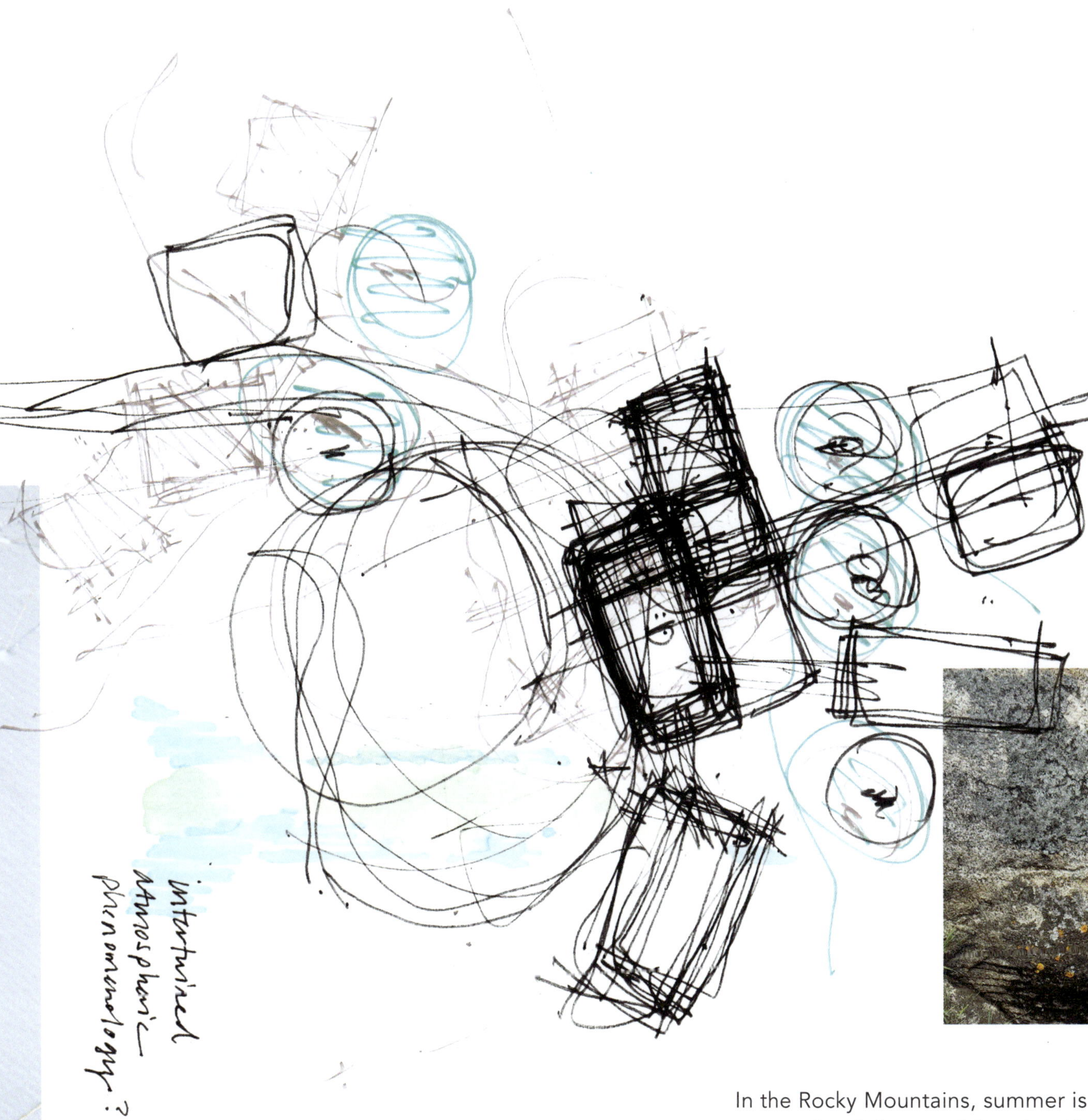

In the Rocky Mountains, summer is a more conventional time to visit a site. Nuances of the topography are more perceptible when unburdened by snow, and longer days invite us to linger, observing gradual shifts in color and light and the locations and complexities of natural features.

Winter, however, offers its own information and magic. The color palette moves toward whites, muted greens, and bark greys. Snowdrifts emphasize the sensual contours of the land, and snowstorms blanket long-range views, guiding our attention to the foreground and emphasizing a scale and composition often overpowered in summer.

We focus initially on topography, access, and sun angles, followed by primary views, the direction of prevailing winds, and potential challenges.

Further inquiry considers more deeply and broadly how to identify and integrate the inherent, tangible qualities embedded within a site: the tones and textures of trees and boulders, seasonal vegetation, secondary views, sounds, wildlife, as well as subjective and metaphorical qualities such as inward-looking or expansiveness.

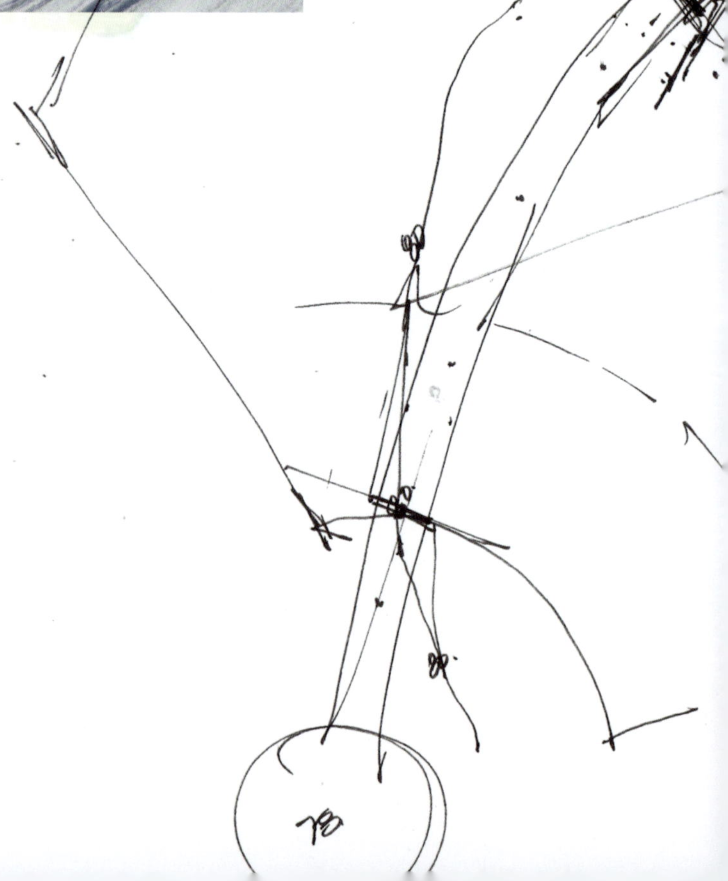

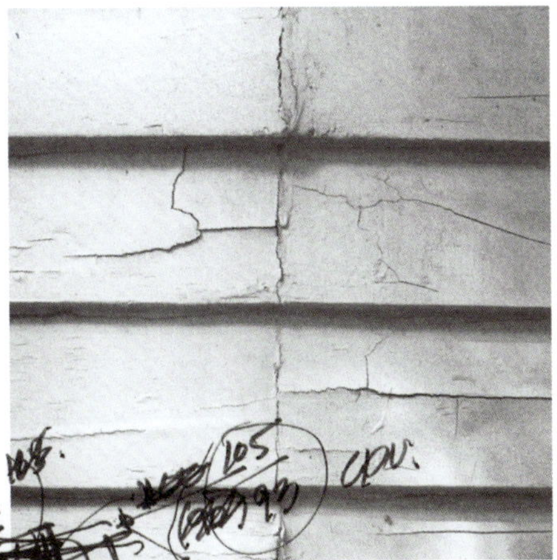

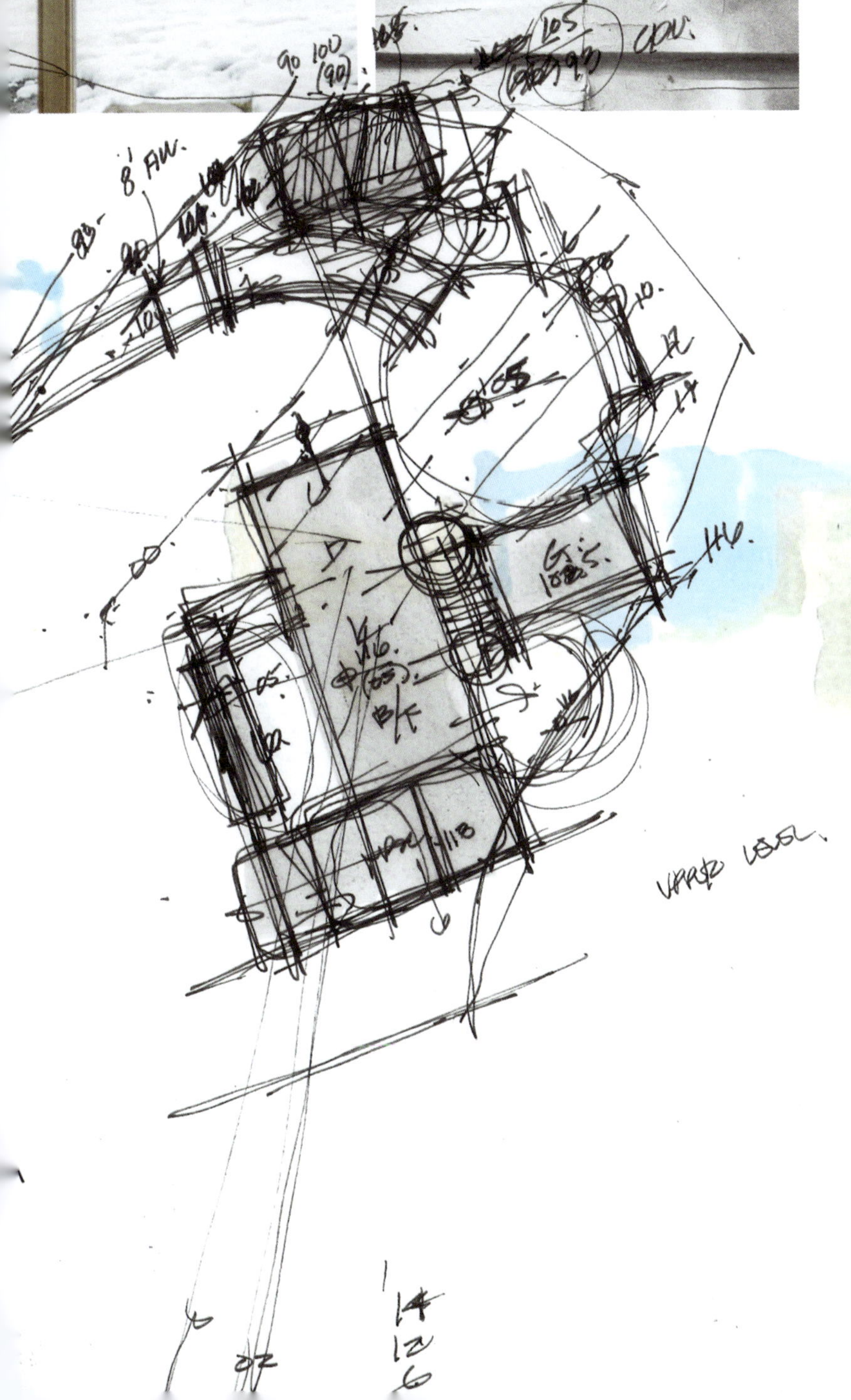

Interviewing a site yields insights in proportion to the interviewer's viewpoint, depth of knowledge, and intuition. When observing the same piece of land, a geologist will identify rock formations and the layers of surrounding landforms, an ornithologist will notice bird habitat, and a hunter can interpret and anticipate wildlife patterns dictated by seasonal changes and the regional landscape.

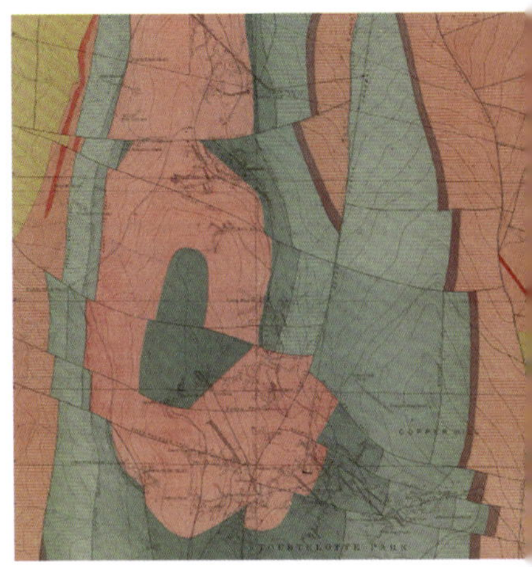

Scientists use ice core samples to understand patterns in climate and temperature; backcountry skiers carefully read the snowpack for similar reasons. They can discern how snow sits on different aspects of a mountain and recognize how wind can load a slope with several times the amount that even a heavy snowfall deposits on a calm day.

That knowledge is important in understanding how snow builds up on a roof or when designing a terrace to be comfortable even in late winter.

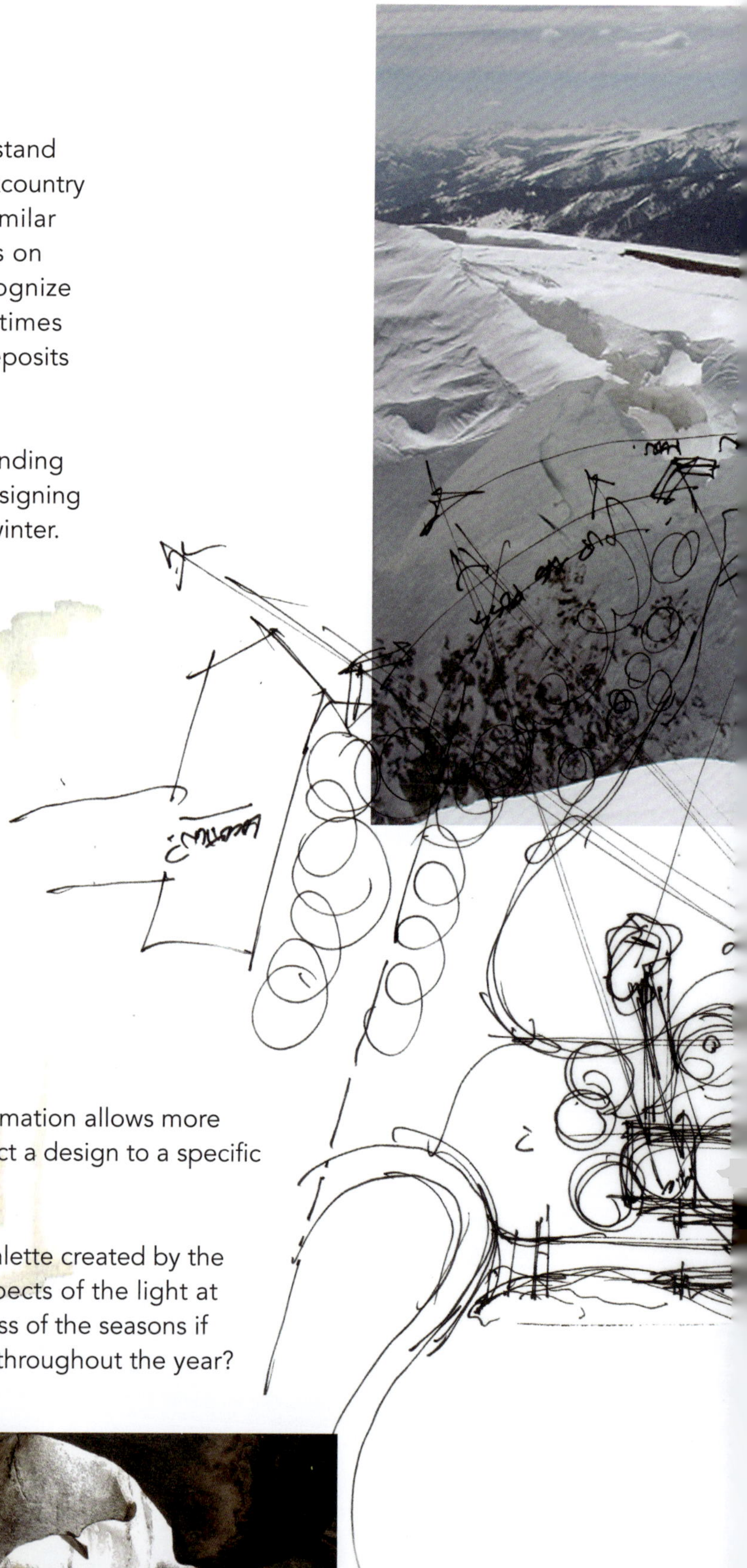

Uncovering a more nuanced grain of information allows more interpretive responses and can also connect a design to a specific place and time.

Can we accentuate a transitioning color palette created by the movement of the sun and shadows or aspects of the light at dawn and dusk? Can we bring an awareness of the seasons if we capture the sound of a river changing throughout the year?

A field of sage, a quintessential western ecosystem, has a beautiful, pungent smell after a rainstorm. Can we create a connection between a living space, region, and weather event by gathering a breeze to infuse a distinctive smell into a house? Investigating these questions can create experiences with dimension and meaning.

Standing in an open meadow, walking in a dense forest, and climbing up to tree house height each allow a unique connection to the land. The environmental aspects of these experiences have a scale to them that can be very large or as small as a window seat; the site dictates the scale of the potential experiences.

Rooms carefully placed on the land to inherit the attributes of a dark forest or the foliage-rich canopy of a tree house can infuse a space with qualities of calm, elation, or spirituality. Weaving these possibilities together with a client's values creates a singular experience of "place," linking together our daily rituals and seasonal time. Sometimes these experiences become extraordinary.

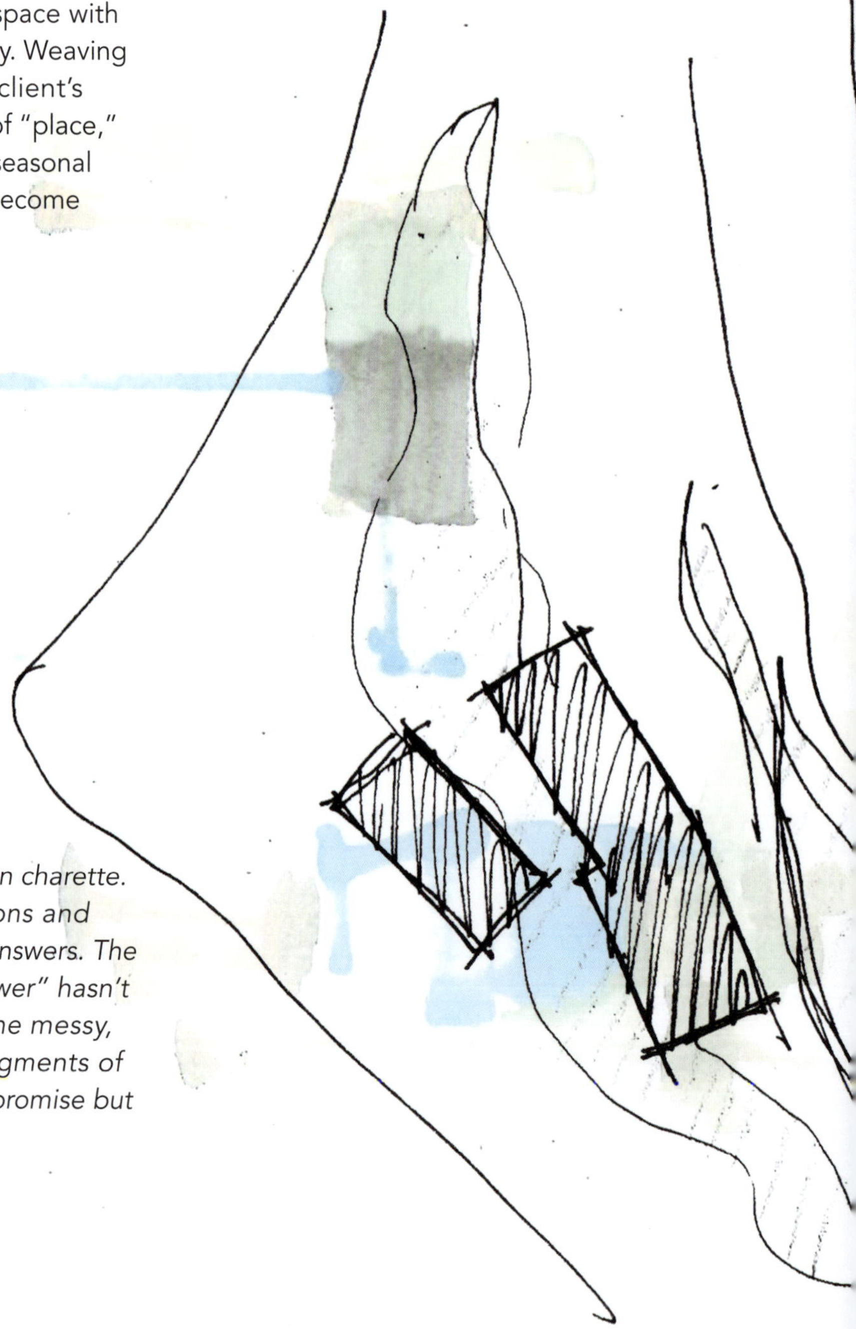

It's early morning, day two of a design charette. As is common at this stage, questions and contradictions outnumber definitive answers. The clients appear worried that "the answer" hasn't appeared. We are accustomed to the messy, iterative charette process where fragments of several sketches and diagrams have promise but don't yet make a whole.

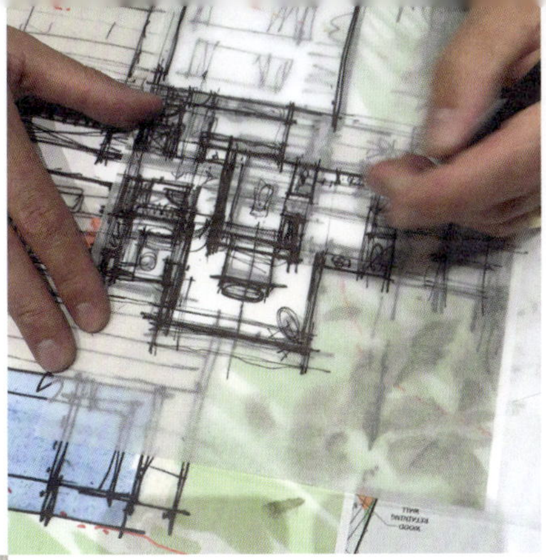

We go back out to the site to test our intuition that, from one location, we might see the Snake River. We bring a ladder and confirm that at about seven feet the river is not only visible but beautifully framed. Maybe this end of the house can hover above the land, freeing the remainder of it to tuck into the site and setting up a choreographed sequence of destinations. The design begins to come together.

CONSERVATION EASEMENT
FLOOD PLAIN
FLOOD PLAIN
WATER
SITE TREES
AREAS OF DENSE VEGETATION
PRIMARY VEHICULAR SITE ACCESS
SECONDARY VEHICULAR SITE ACCESS
HUNTER CREEK TRAIL
HUNTER CREEK SITE ACCESS, TBD
LOT 4 ACCESS, VIA EASEMENT

Meadow

07 25

DBX, Colorado
4.9 Acres
The Meadow
Not Piggish
Bent Can
Un-Precious
How We Live
Pushing Rules
The Miniatures
15% 85%
Precise Separation
Water Sound
Surprise Light
And I Love It
Pug Palace
Because It's Fun

06 18

The building site is a meadow that was part of a working ranch. Below it, a small river can be heard but not seen. The gregarious owners wanted a comfortable, casual environment for gathering their numerous friends and family. The extensive program includes five guest bedrooms, a theater, and a bowling alley. The owners challenged us to make the house appear as small as possible; we challenged ourselves to be light on the land.

Analyzing the site revealed that a significant percentage of the program could be inserted under the meadow and capture the sounds of the river below. The alluring sound of the water helped the owners embrace locating guest bedrooms predominantly below grade. Continuing the idea, an upper meadow is extended over the primary suite and support spaces, tucked under a planted roof.

The result is that only the living areas and an office—quiet forms that open subtly—appear as the house's built expression. The living room roof creates a scoop for the sounds of the river, bringing them deep inside. The office mirrors the living room, opening to the south. On approach, this small structure, set in native grasses, is all that is visible, revealing itself as part of a larger composition only from the auto court.

The areas anchored into the meadow are cast-on-site concrete panels that contrast with the dark charred wood that clads the rest of the complex. Glass and steel accents complete the material palette. In the primary suite, skylights bring light through the planted roof, grazing walls and creating a soothing counterbalance to the large windows.

This house lives large, but its visual expression is minimal and evocative. And by partially embedding into the land, it respects and enhances the original meadow.

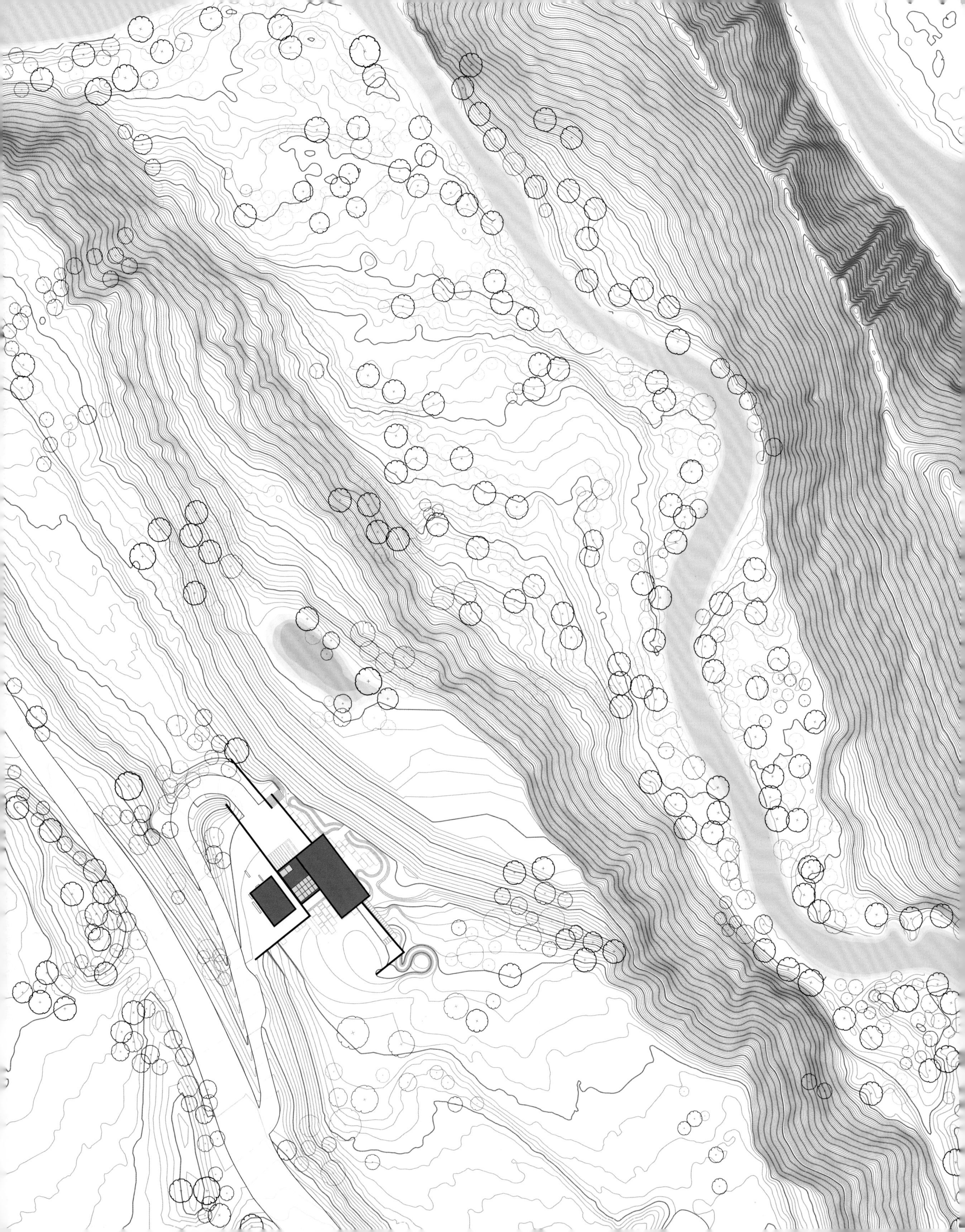

The office, seen from ranch road.

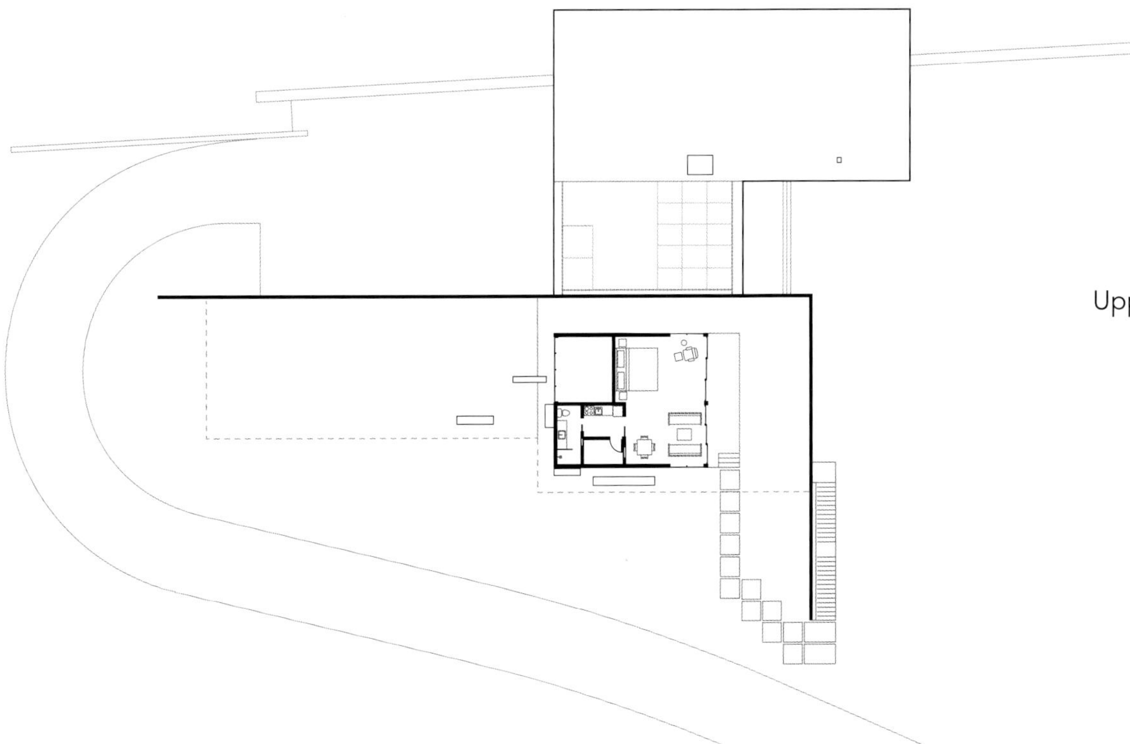

Upper Level

Main Level

Opposite: Snow lingers on a primary bath skylight.

Right: A strip of window marks the intersection of the living areas with the concrete-clad spaces tucked under the meadow.

SUNSET THAT SCREENS, REVEALS

Top opposite: The concrete stair is anchored up to the landing and transitions to wood treads which float up to the entry. The openness brings borrowed light deep into the lower level.

Bottom opposite: Primary materials—concrete, steel, and charred wood—come together at a fireplace in the rec room.

Top right: The entry forms a bridge-like waist that connects the living spaces with the primary suite.

Bottom right: A glass roof at the outdoor room is visible from the stairway.

An east-facing deck off the dining area orients toward the butte and collects sounds of the river below.

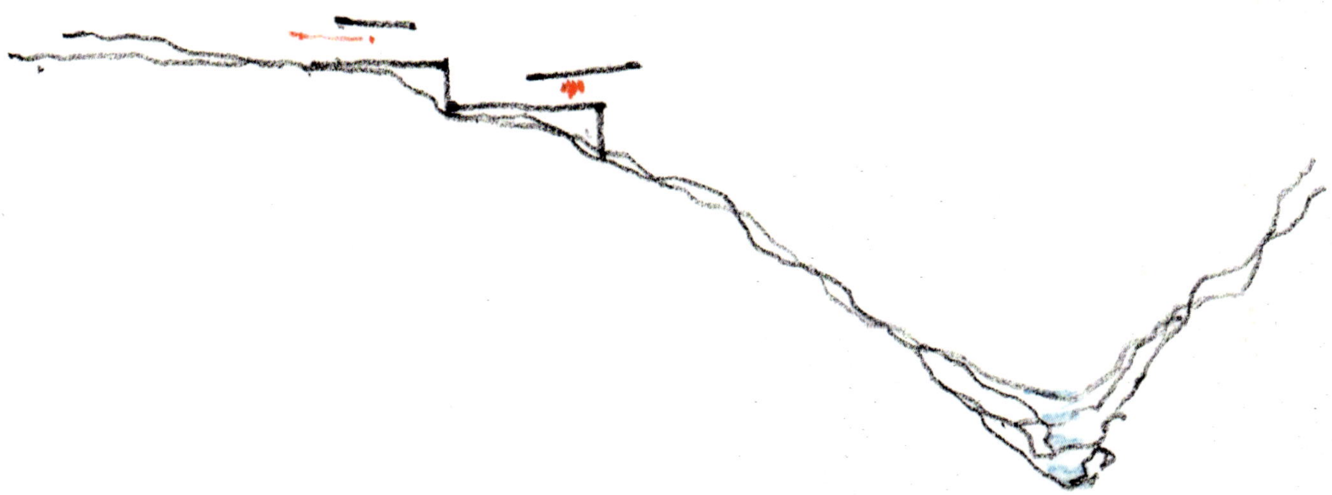

Red Butte

06 15

Aspen, Colorado
1980s
Response to Constraints
Street Relationship
1.6 Acres
90 Linear Feet
Geology
Capture the Ridgeline
Two Things
Aspen Beach
Filtered Light
Organic Relief
The Card Room
Surface Anneal
Six Butterflies
This Is What We Do

06 01

The owners wished to transform an older residence into a sophisticated but casual home with expanded living space for their family and visitors. The husband, a geologist, also wanted to strengthen the connection to Red Butte, a rusty-red landform behind the house that rises almost 500 feet above the valley floor.

A city ordinance mandating that new construction take place only within the existing home's footprint posed a considerable challenge for increasing the program but allowed mature trees surrounding the house to remain as a privacy buffer from nearby neighbors.

Expanding the living space takes two forms—one perceptual and one physical. Although the main level couldn't be physically enlarged, the rooms are conceptually expanded by dissolving the exterior walls and allowing the expanse of nature beyond to define the spaces. And, by excavating below the existing structure, the house is enlarged to include subgrade entertainment areas.

Large windows and stacking doors on three sides open to an aspen and evergreen grove, defining the perceived boundaries of the living, dining, and kitchen spaces. Wraparound decks—part of the existing house enjoyed by the owners—are retained for coffee in the morning or a glass of wine in the evening. On the northwest corner of the house, the primary bedroom is dramatically eroded and Red Butte itself seems to be one of the bedroom walls, catching and reflecting sunlight from early morning until sundown.

The architectural forms are quiet and pared down in their expression. De-emphasizing the architecture highlights the surrounding nature as well as the reclaimed elm and oak's subtle textural shifts on the interior surfaces and cabinetry.

The filtered light coming through the trees is reinterpreted in wood trellises; like the trees, the trellises provide privacy in places where it is called for and, in others, simply the sensory pleasure of dappled light. The wood's natural tone-on-tone finishes underscore the warm, casual environment where people take center stage for this gregarious, fun-loving family.

MATERIAL WORLD

Previous and current spreads: The white oak screen at the front door is repeated inside the entry, animating the space and tying the two levels together. It allows filtered light into what would otherwise be a back-of-house hallway.

Previous and current spreads: Reclaimed elm is used on walls as well as the primary cabinetry. The wood's texture gives the spare forms a quiet richness. White oak is used for secondary cabinetry and benches, creating a tone-on-tone wood expression.

Connecting

These projects demonstrate the opportunities made possible when unusual or challenging site characteristics are elevated and combine powerfully and artfully with the aspirations of the owner. They illustrate how the values of client and site can come together to create an experience greater than the sum of the parts.

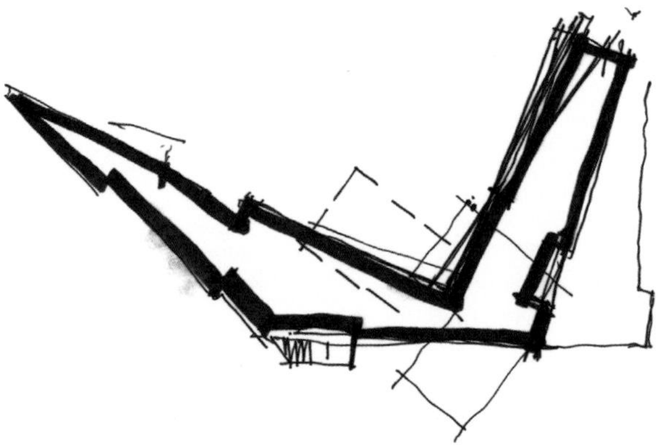

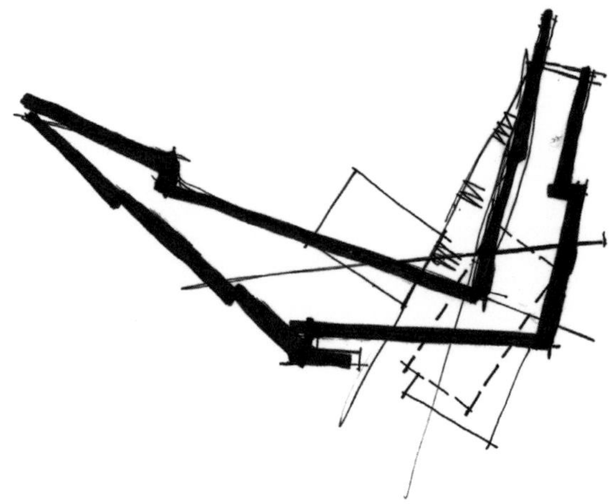

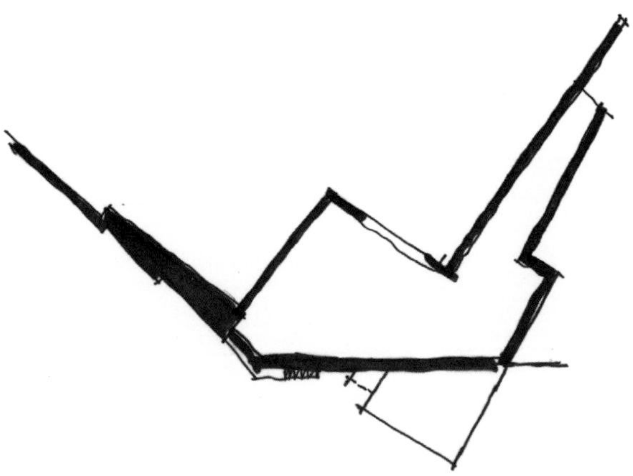

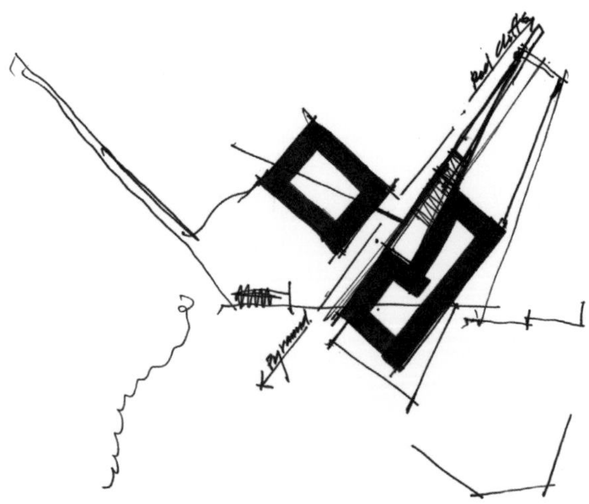

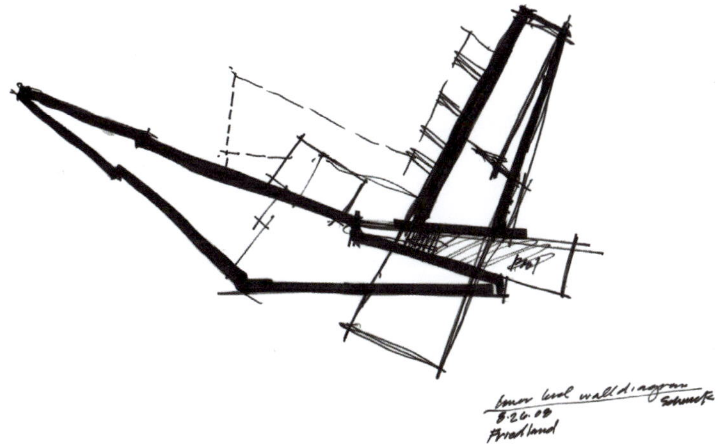
lower level wall diagram
8.26.08

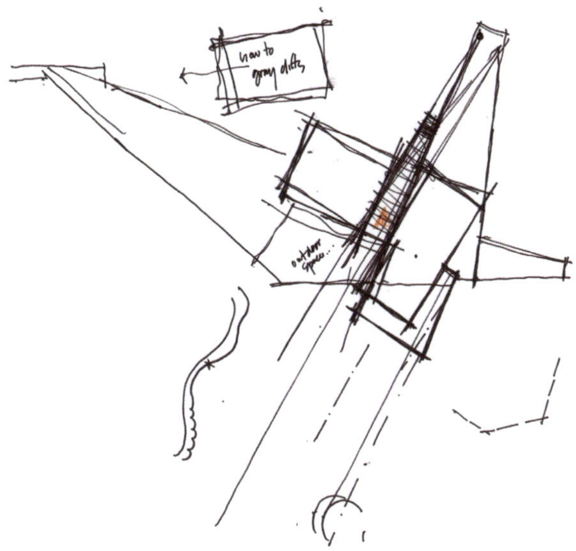

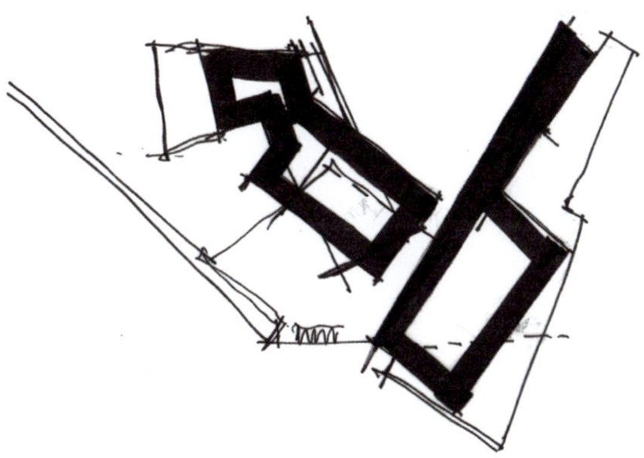

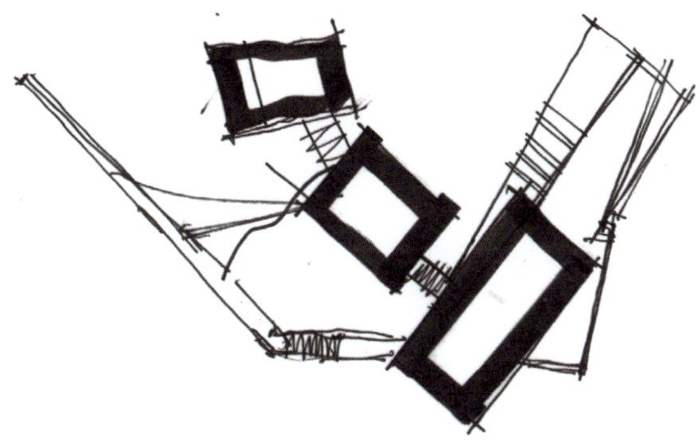

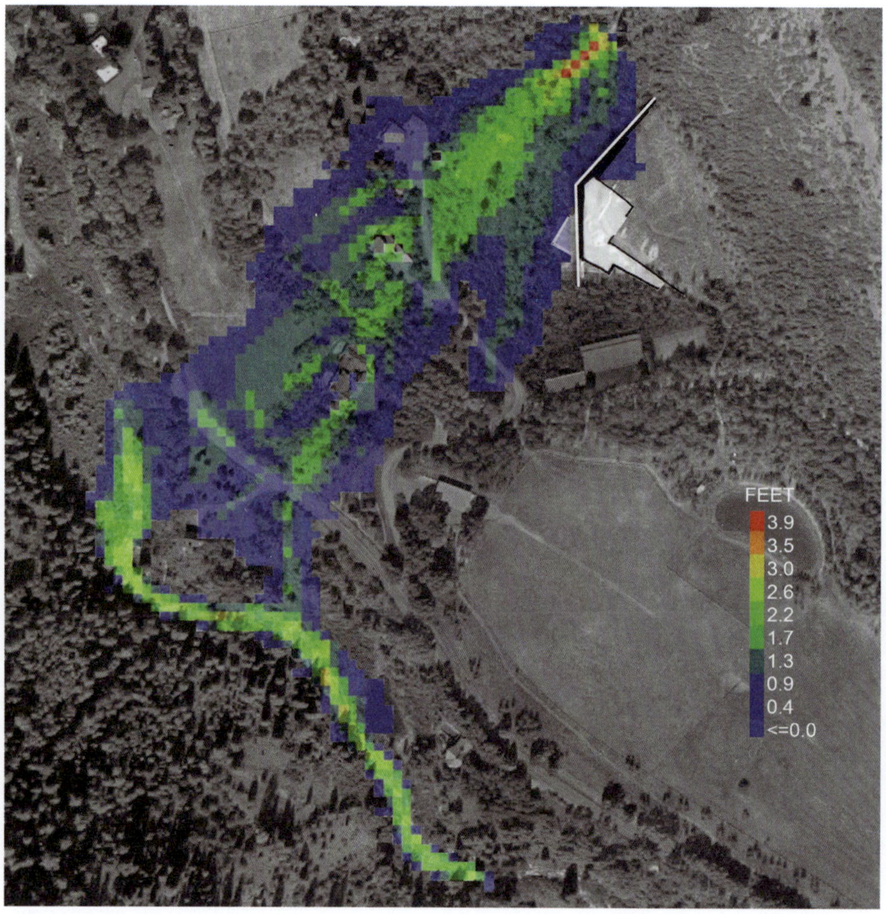

Wall House

This visually dynamic site, with its steep topography and eroded red-rock cliffs above, has a constrained building envelope subject to substantial debris flows. Within this context, the owner wished to maximize views to Pyramid Peak, as it reminds him of a favorite pilgrimage destination in India.

The required debris-resistant walls are substantial. Taking a cue from memorable structures like the Great Wall of China, the design investigates making a three-dimensional construct of the structural requirements and interpreting it into forms that can be inhabited inside and out—with rooms, terraces, and more intimate spaces. The walls, embedded in the earth, are also living space, blurring the distinction between site and architecture.

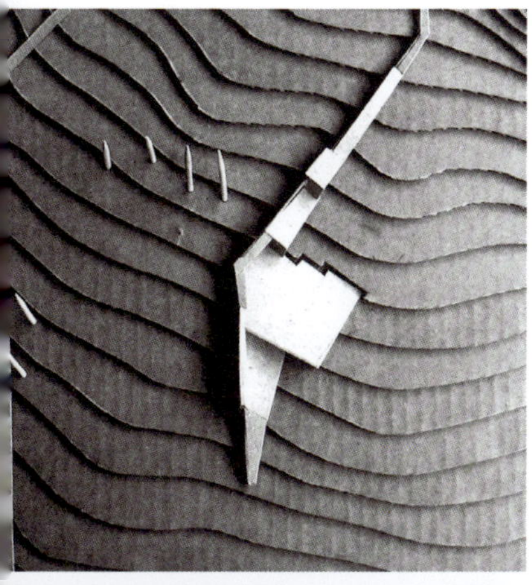

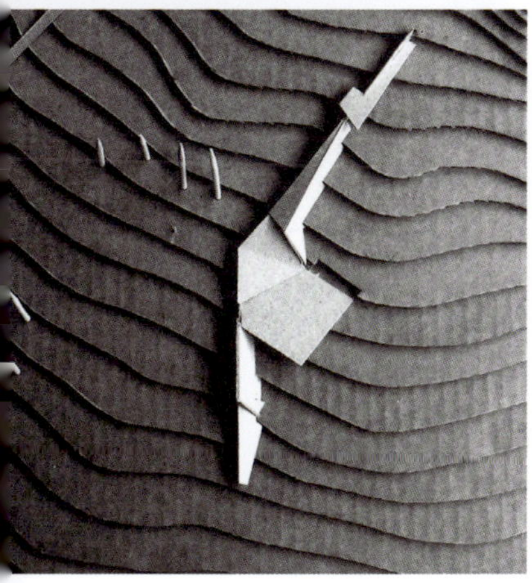

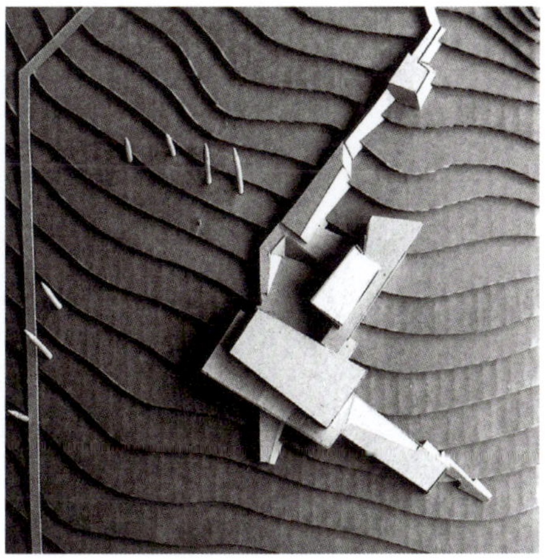

Contrasting with the anchoring elements, zinc pavilions hold the remainder of the program in crisply detailed directional forms. The living pavilion creates a picture frame around Pyramid Peak, editing out other views. At the upper edge of the property, a meditation retreat called the Zendo creates one more homage to Pyramid—a plunge pool reflecting the peak.

The design accepts exposure to the elements, expressed in the protective walls, and translates that exposure into living space. The house is rooted in the earth and also visually assertive in its environment, echoing the geological qualities of the land and nearby cliffs. In the event of a debris flow, assertiveness is an appropriate response for this site.

Previous spread: Early sketches of interpreting the wall as living space.

Aperture

The owners have an affinity for the photographs of Lindsey Ross, a Telluride artist, whose work will hang in the completed house. Their remote site sits at the bottom of a deep canyon.

Due to the steep, mountainous terrain, it became important to clarify the house's location by establishing a relationship with distant ridgelines. The ridgelines, site, and artwork informed a choreographed decompression sequence from the entrance to a memorable living space.

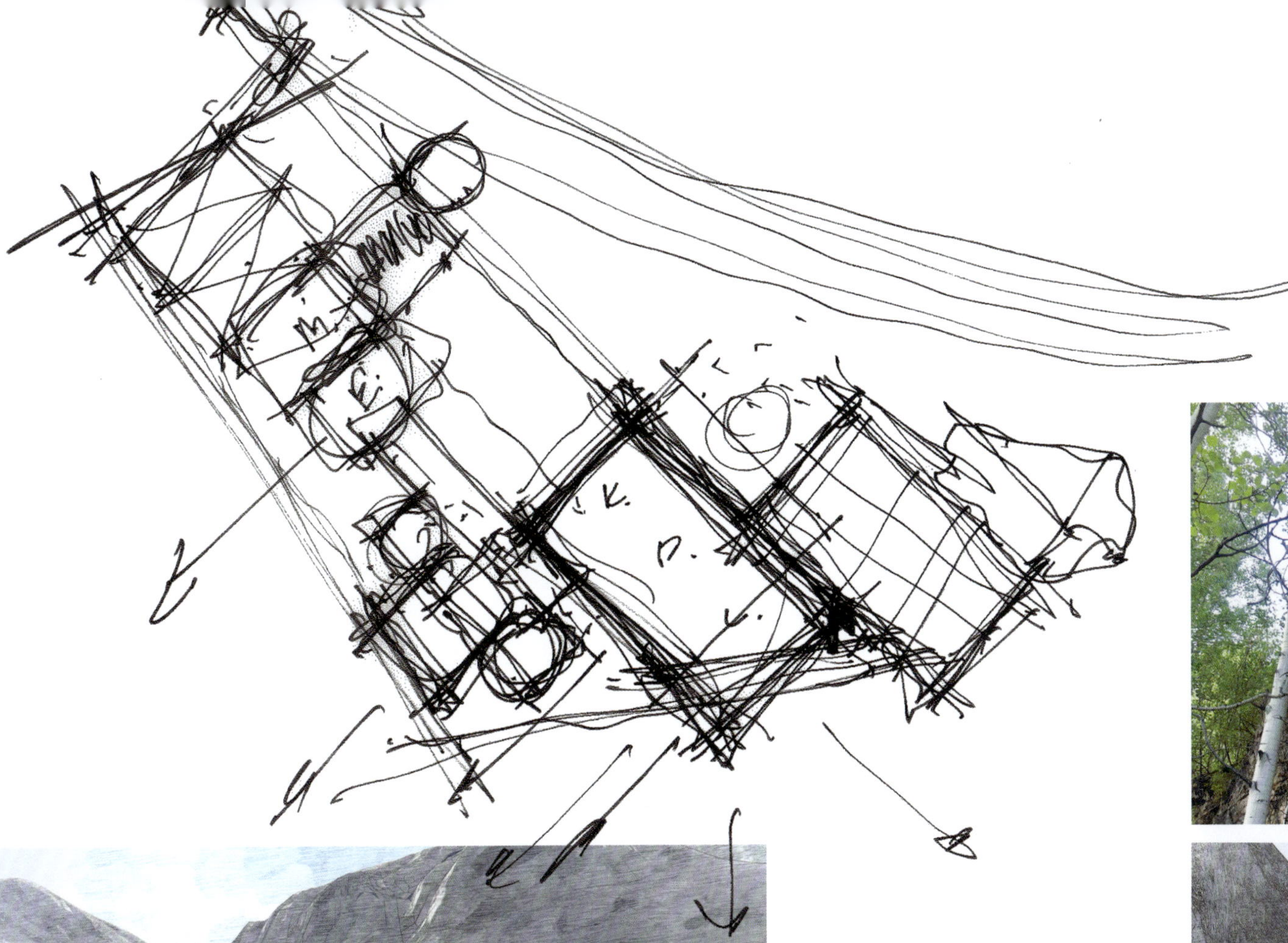

At the entry, a slice of mountain and sky, cropped like a photograph by a jutting light monitor, draws you into the house. As you approach the view, another light monitor captures a snapshot of a second ridgeline, turning you ninety degrees and pulling you toward the living spaces.

The third movement and final destination in the choreography leads to a massive boulder, a twenty-foot-high fragment of the mountain that anchors an outdoor room. The striking presence of the tangible boulder vividly contrasts with distant views, awakening the senses at journey's end.

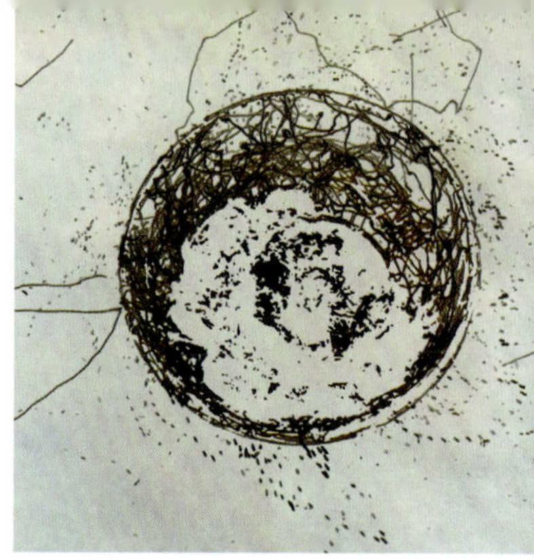

Telluride Transfer

Telluride's picturesque downtown is a National Historic Landmark District. The community's commitment to preserve the built environment and connect to nature is at the center of its shared cultural values. These values became the guiding principles for a complex that includes a community art center, affordable and market housing, and retail space.

In many ways, Telluride's alleys exemplify the attitudes embraced by this community. These active pathways and meeting places have a rugged vitality and offer glimpses of nature; they are ad hoc and a little bit gritty.

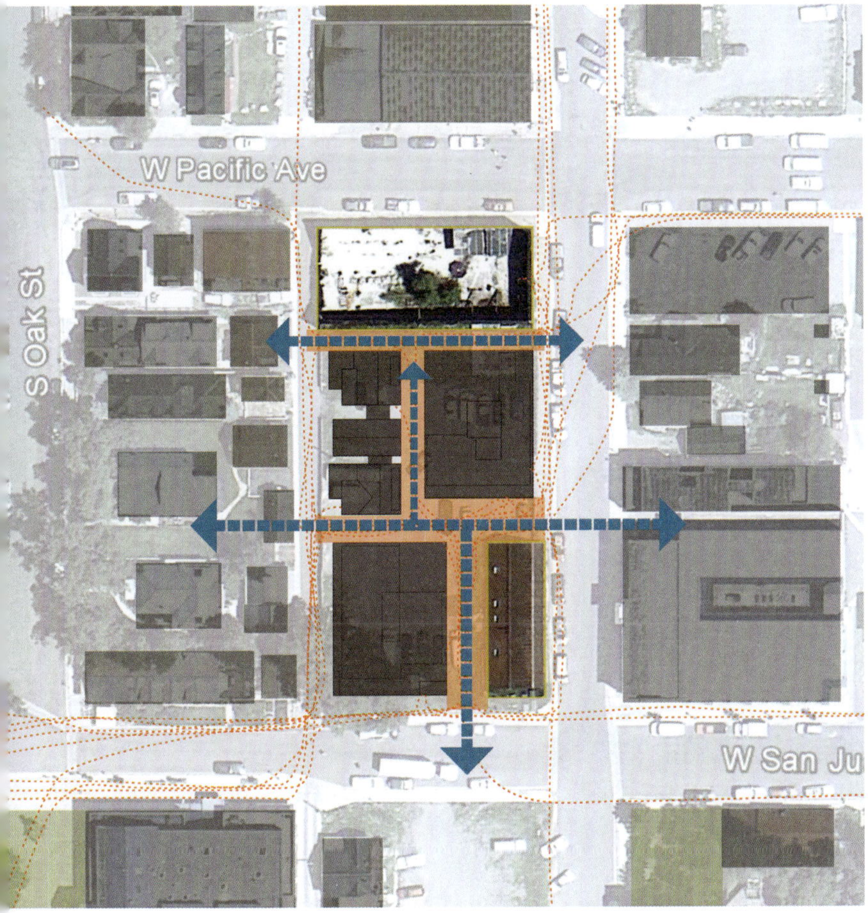

The master plan seamlessly integrates with the town's existing fabric, accommodating current footpaths and alleys and giving equal importance to the spaces in between buildings—the new alleys—as to the buildings themselves. The buildings preserve pedestrian connections and create apertures to sunlight and peaks.

Consistent with the goals, the buildings' forms blend into the town rather than assert themselves. They draw attention only at a more detailed level, combining corrugated zinc and an unexpectedly dark brick, laid up to dematerialize as it reflects changing sunlight.

In the best sense, it is difficult to identify the complex as "a project." The cultural values shared by the community drove the approach of this integrated, smart, and livable design that is wholly adapted to its site.

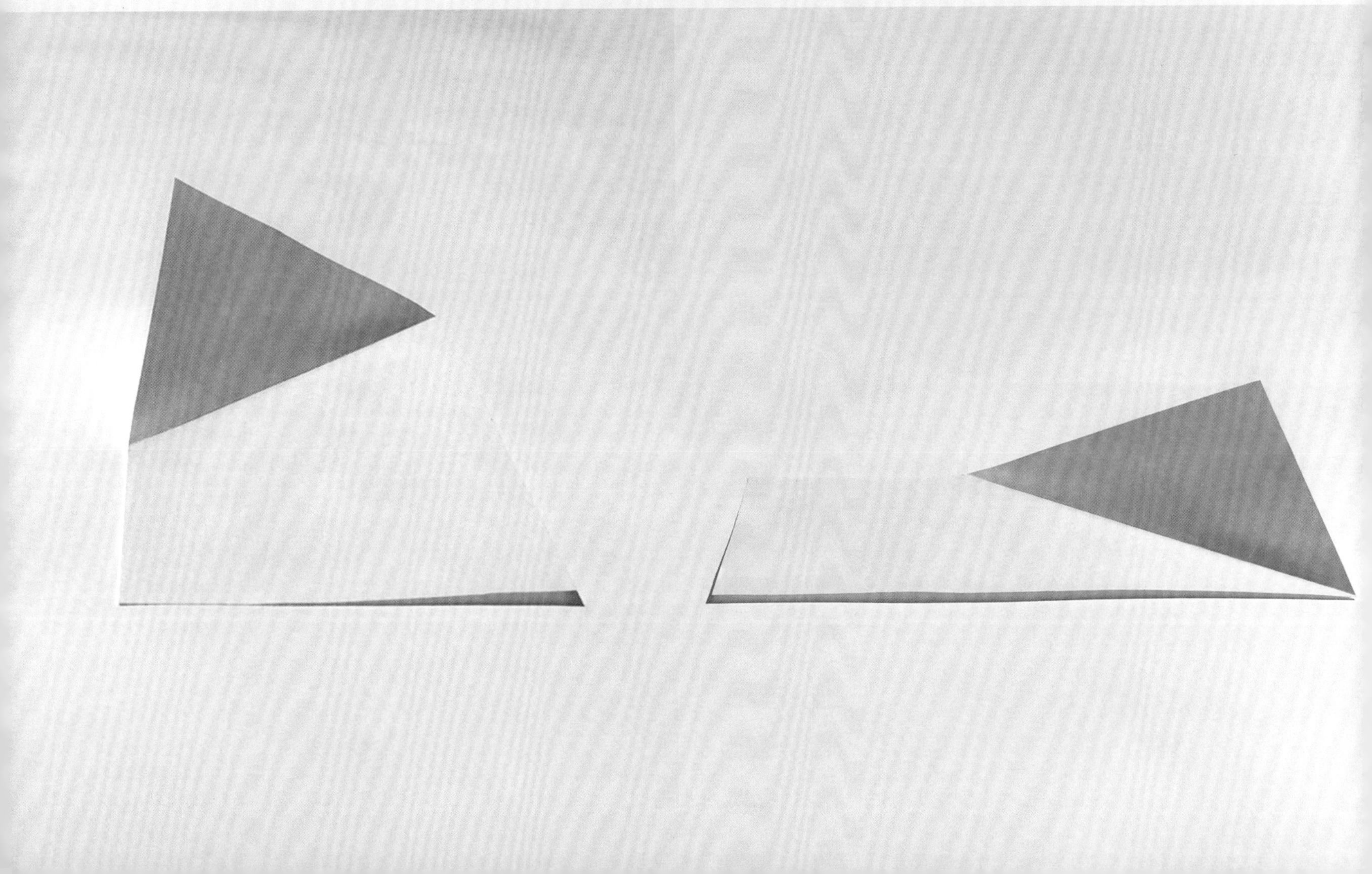

DNA Alpine

The clients are committed stewards of this large parcel of wild land. They wanted a small artful house and identified its specific location: the edge of a slight depression in the landscape that forms a subtle bowl, backed by towering trees. Their further requirements—that all existing trees be saved and the bowl remain in its natural state—resulted in a very small footprint.

The design embraces smallness and deference to the land. Dividing the program into three buildings allowed each to adapt to the topography and fit between the trees to form a loose compound connected with walking paths.

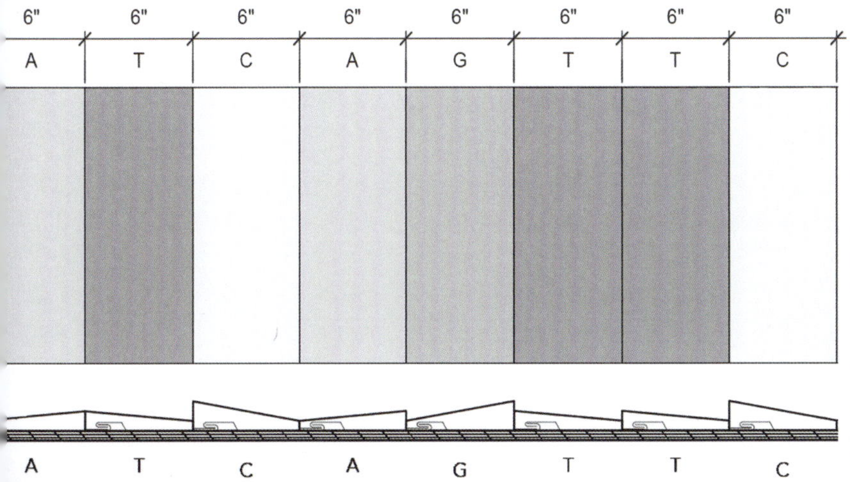

Compressing the form and making the house as small as possible resulted in a folded roof plane, pulled down to reduce volume, and a sinuous elevation which follows topography. At its tallest, the house is less than half the height of the trees behind it.

For cladding, copper sheeting was formed into four profiles which could be used in any pattern. In a nod to the husband, whose field is synthetic biology, the pattern is the DNA sequence of a heritage Engelmann spruce behind the house. The non-repetitive sequence wraps continuously around the structure. The siding's shifting, slightly reflective patterns create an interactive experience on the site—a dynamic camouflage in changing daylight, which will continue to patina with each passing season.

The design is modest and subservient, allowing the site to remain a sanctuary. The DNA sequence, ever present and unseen, underscores the subtleties of the landscape and the beauty of deferring to it.

Previous spread: Paper parti studies of folded roofs.

Next spread: The unfolded elevation follows the topography. The DNA sequence of Engelmann spruce is applied to exterior siding.

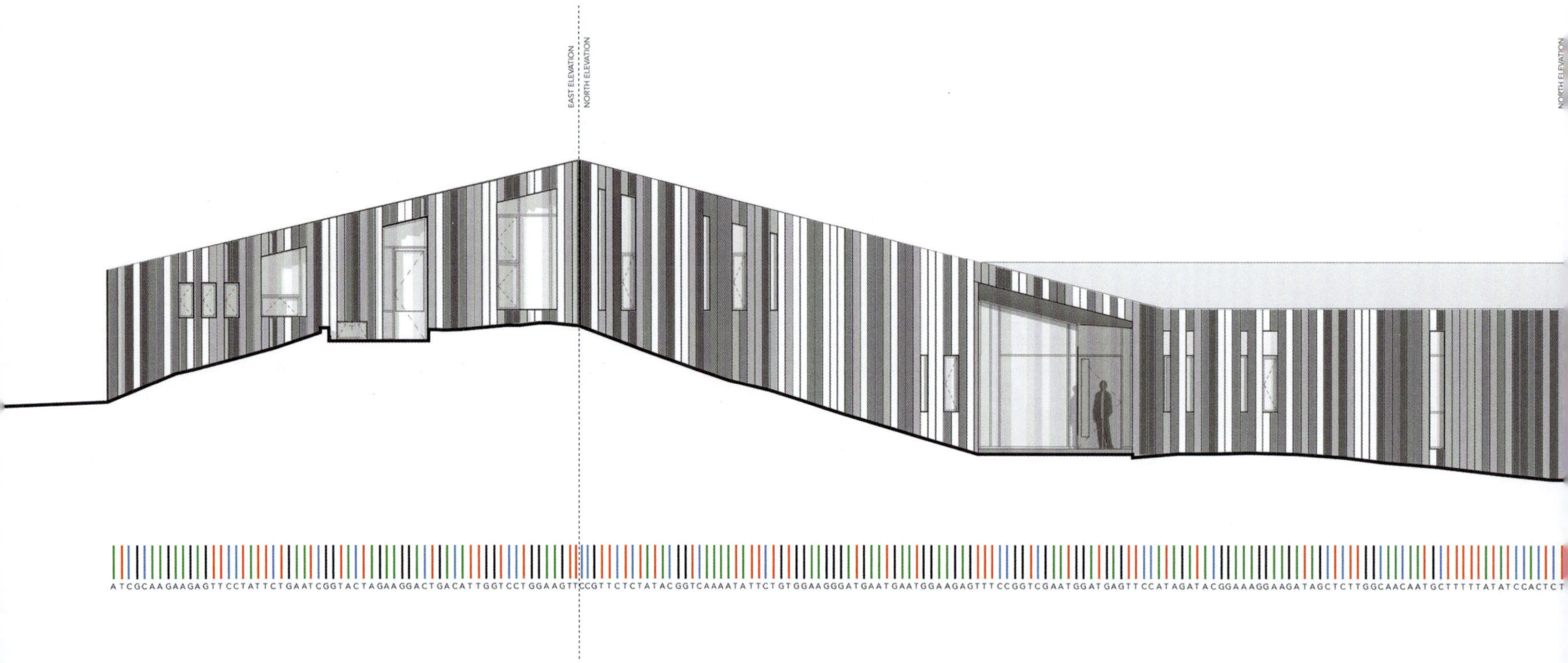
EAST ELEVATION
NORTH ELEVATION
NORTH ELEVATION
ATCGCAAGAAGAGTTCCTATTCTGAATCGGTACTAGAAGGACTGACATTGGTCCTGGAAGTTCCGTTCTCTATACGGTCAAAATATTCTGTGGAAGGGATGAATGAATGGAAGAGTTTCCGGTCGAATGGATGAGTTCCATAGATACGGAAAGGAAGATAGCTCTTGGCAACAATGCTTTTTATATCCACTCT

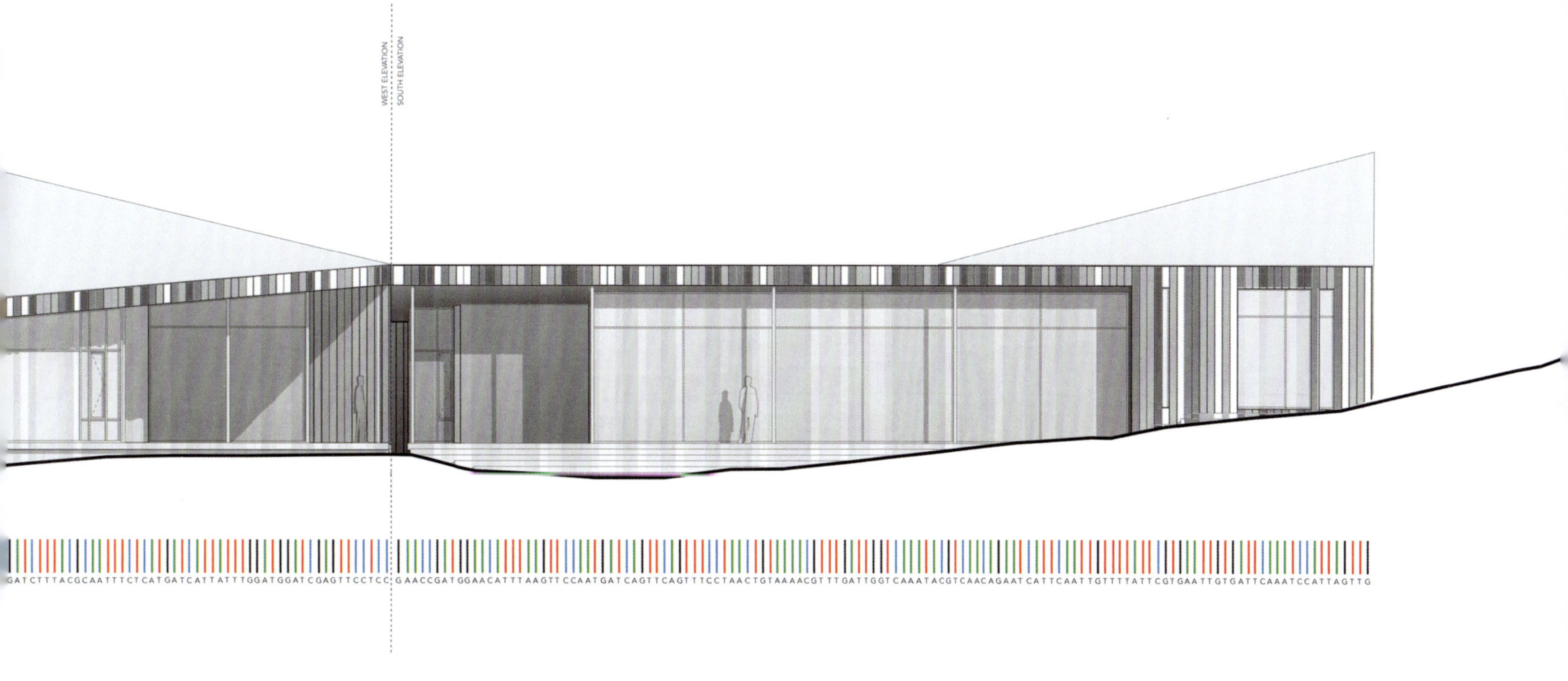
WEST ELEVATION
SOUTH ELEVATION
GATCTTTACGCAATTTCTCATGATCATTATTTGGATGGATCGAGTTCCTCC
GAACCGATGGAACATTTAAGTTCCAATGATCAGTTCAGTTTCCTAACTGTAAAACGTTTGATTGGTCAAATACGTCAACAGAATCATTCAATTGTTTTATTCGTGAATTGTGATTCAAATCCATTAGTTG

Bridge

07 21

Eagle County, Colorado
4.83 Acres
Bending to Nature
Around the Trees
Gable Vignette
Editing Forms
2 Buttresses
1 Wing
Continuous Coursing
Flitches Upon Flitches
Refined and Effortless
Why, It's Lovely
There Was a Reason
Art Stories
A Forest Runs Through It

12 15

The challenge for the house was twofold. The owners envisioned their art collection in a thoroughly modern "steel-and-glass pavilion" in a community with more traditional design requirements, including gable roofs for all houses. And, they wished to preserve a beautiful, mature aspen grove on the site.

Typical construction would cut off drainage to the aspens downhill, damaging the forest and potentially killing many trees. The solution for preserving the grove came out of working with the topography: rather than build on the site, the main level is lifted up to bridge over a slight swale, preserving critical drainage patterns and allowing the forest floor to flow beneath.

From the entry courtyard this glassy bridge gives a veiled hint of the larger landscape beyond. It houses living and dining spaces, while the "buttresses" on either end have the required roof forms and the balance of the house's program. The bridge is quiet on the approach side and opens up with a winglike form to the south. With its sectional qualities and transparent walls, space flows unimpeded through it, projecting dramatically toward long southern views.

The lower north roof establishes a secondary plane which runs through the house, knitting together the gables and bridge. Rooms within the gables are more conventionally defined in section and fenestration and form intimate contrasts to the bridge's openness. Pennsylvania bluestone, steel, cedar, and walnut thread their way throughout the house.

The gables are a calm fit within the community context, and their expected nature sets up the contrasting, dynamic bridge in the forest.

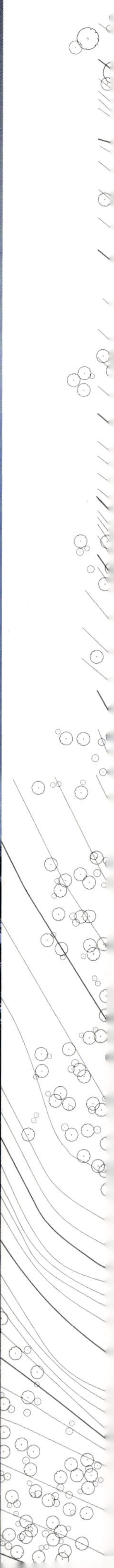

Opposite: Freestanding integral sinks on a steel base create his-and-hers vanities with circulation all around to help create a forest-immersed space with spa-like qualities.

Above: An outdoor dining room perched in the tree canopy has a glazed corner to deflect occasional wind gusts.

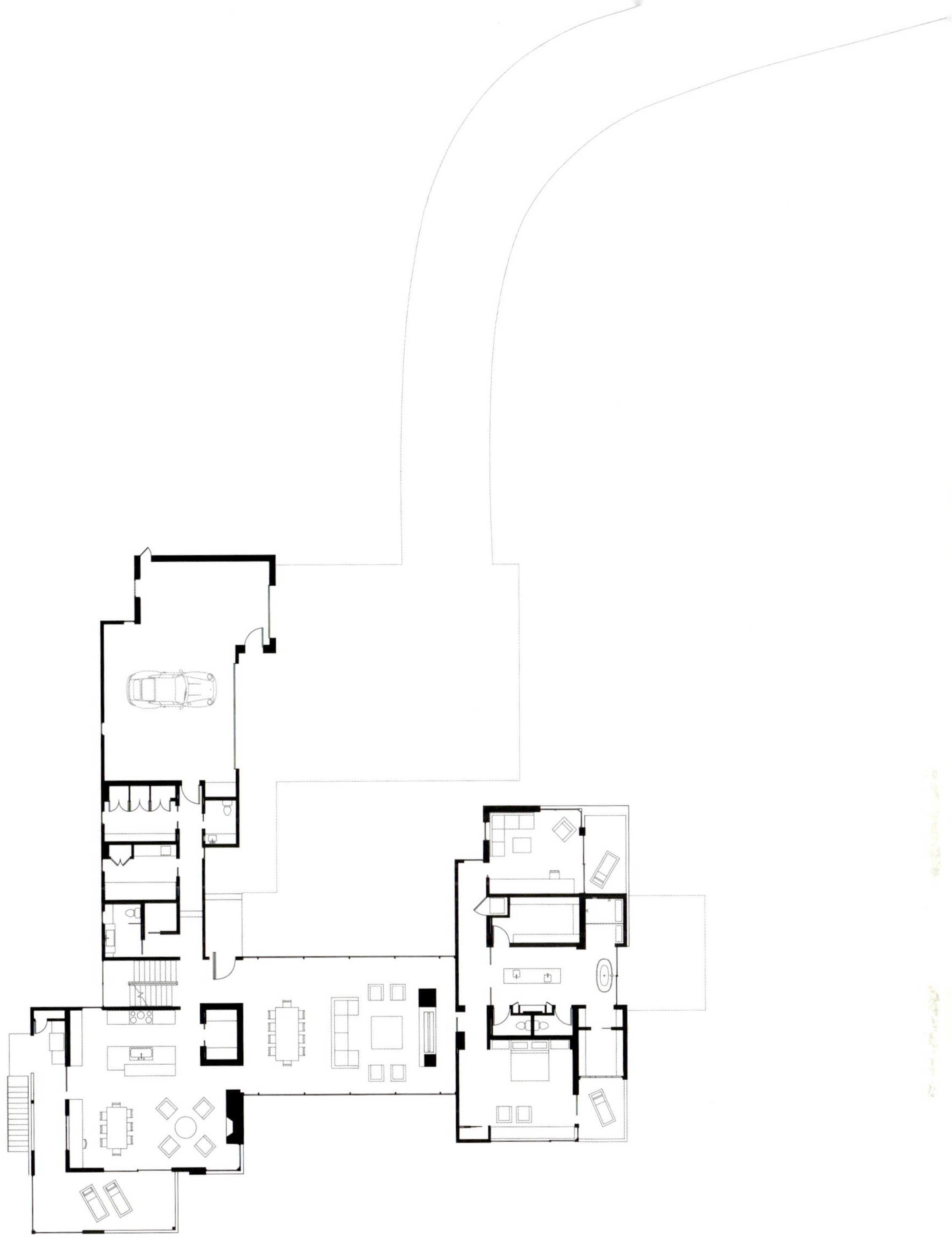

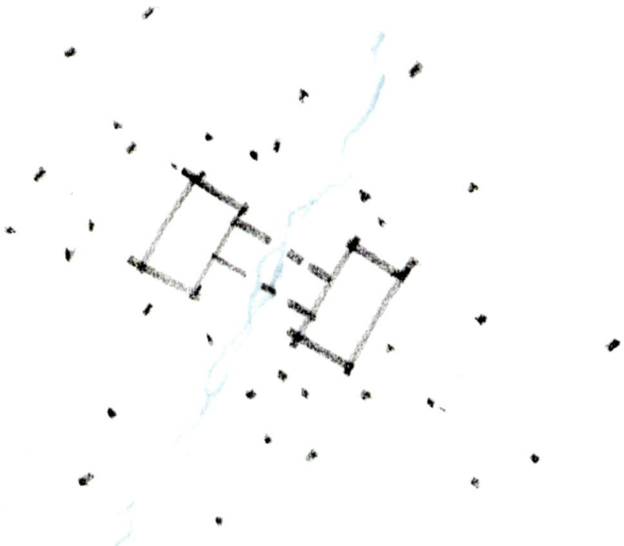

Maroon Creek Overlook

12 12

Aspen, Colorado
2.47 Acres
The Creek
The Bridge
The Saddle
Pushing the Edge
360°
Great Lawn
Zen Nooks
Pockets of Architecture
Carved Corners
Inside-Out Contrast
Cantilevered Moments
From Subtle to Daring

10 07

A couple with young children asked for a contemporary living environment with distinct areas for living, primary suite, and children's bedrooms.

The building envelope is a subtle bowl at the edge of a steep hillside which drops abruptly to an alpine stream flowing through the valley below. The stream is a gorgeous amenity, but real views of it are difficult because of the steep angle to the valley floor 110 feet below the house site. Other challenges include a nearby road and active bike path which require privacy considerations.

The house is conceived as three pods on the edge of the drop-off, each containing one of the program elements, connected by transparent links. The pods push, pull, and rotate, relative to the edge, to tuck into the bowl and capture the inherent drama of the land.

The pods are beveled forms with eroded corners, cantilevering over solid bases. The beveled roofs are quiet in the landscape while the lifted cantilevers accentuate the drop in the site, creating dramatic living spaces perched out over the hillside. The open corners encourage diagonal viewing to the valley and streambed below, counteracting the steep angle straight downhill.

The pushing and pulling of the masses also create pockets of privacy; an outdoor room and lawn, located to capture full-day sun, are carved into the site and enclosed by architectural concrete walls. The enclosure creates added privacy from the adjacent bike path. Native vegetation extends to the edge of the site walls, creating a Zen-like oasis in the landscape.

The muted tones and quiet forms of the exterior are a foil to the bold and playful interiors, expressing the owners' interests in contemporary art and fashion.

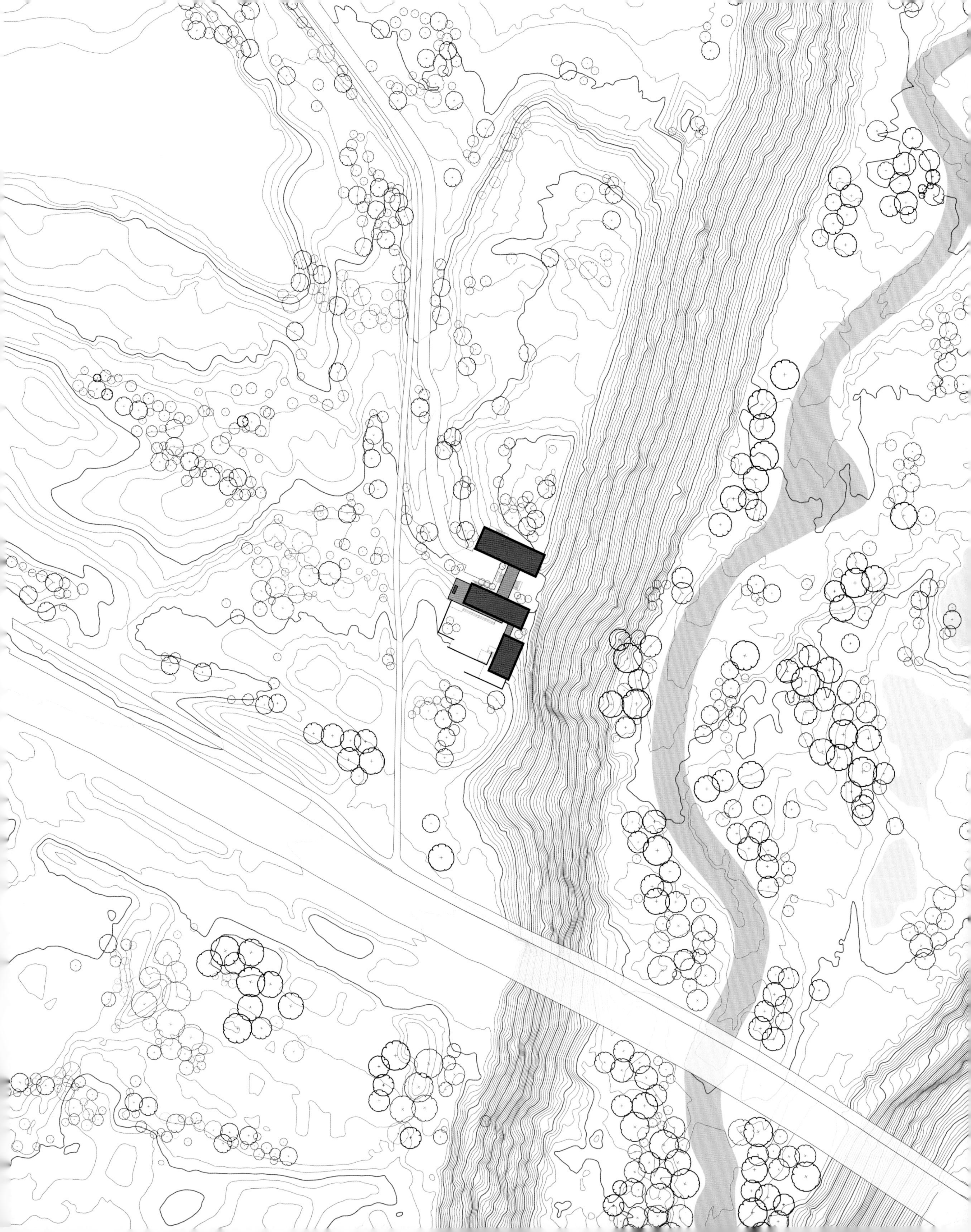

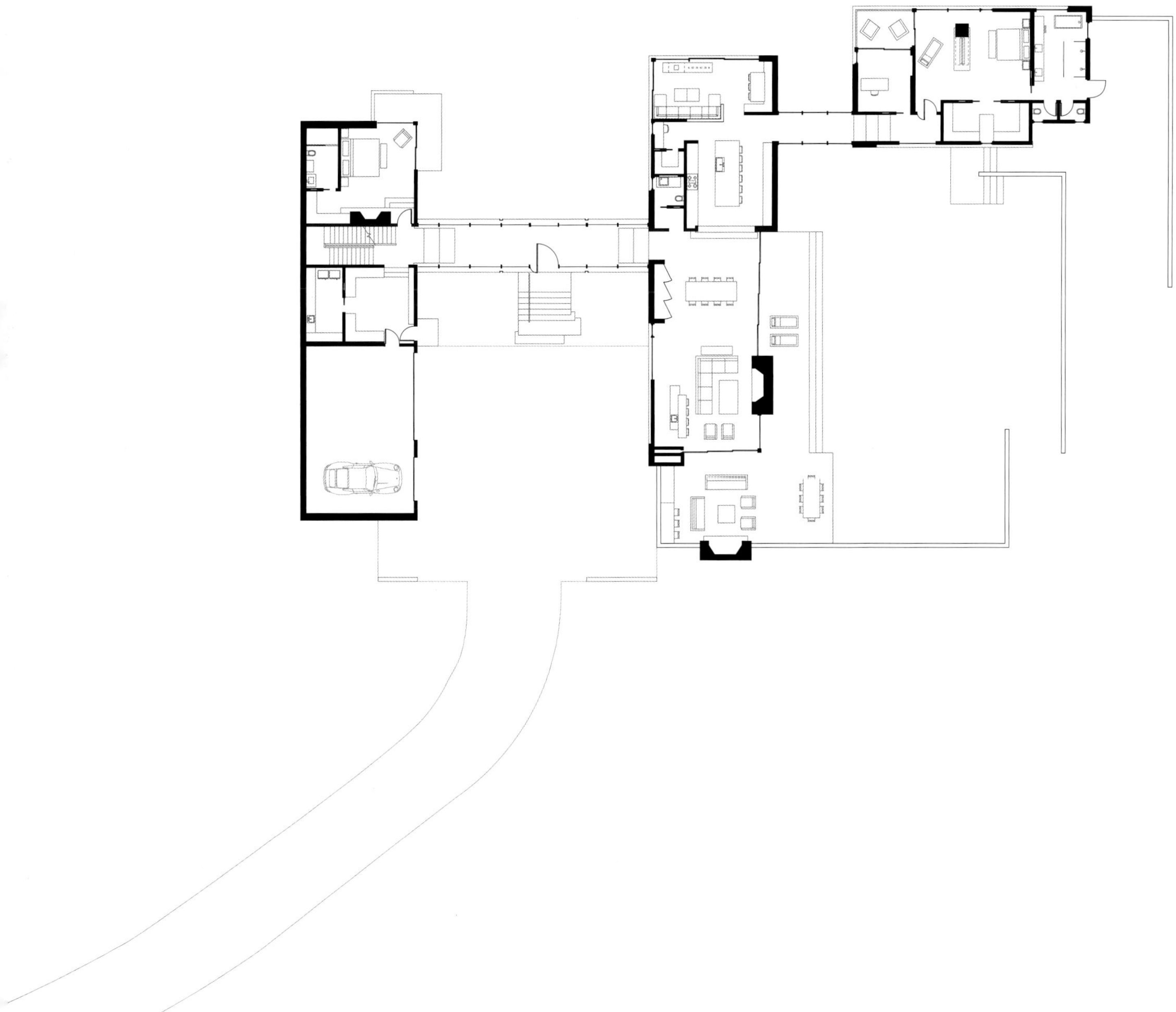

In the cozy family room, the two-sided fireplace glass reveals unexpected glimpses of the ravine below.

Red Mountain

11 21

Aspen, Colorado
.82 Acres
Defying Suburban
Intricacy
Activist
Constraint
Concrete to the Table
Screen Out
Deconstructivist
Volumes and Planes
Anchor and Hillside
Pivot
Living and Recreating
Transition

06 05

AMI
A MAN
I AM
THE MAN

The owners wished to integrate their collection of art and photography related to the civil rights movement into a house with a strong design sensibility and an equally strong connection to "nature's art" outside.

Situated on a street in close proximity to its neighbors, the house is a layered composition of architectural walls used to shield neighbors, guide movement, and create private outdoor spaces. Walls are occasionally fragmented, sequentially obstructing and then revealing unexpected moments throughout the house.

The primary material palette for exterior and interior surfaces is board-formed concrete, glass, and two grey/black materials: blackened steel and a high-density fiberboard cladding. The cladding is more prevalent on the exterior for its weathering capabilities and the steel more prevalent on the interior, but the two materials are purposefully overlapped to create a rich, shadowy foil to the lighter concrete and glass. Inside, the dark color palette is extended with black smoked oak floors and ceilings, espresso-stained custom millwork, as well as steel panels with a more refined finish.

The sculptural quality of the architecture is expressed in the home's three fireplaces, each one unique. As a centerpiece separating the kitchen from the living room, a two-sided fireplace summarizes the materiality of the home and the continuity of its design spirit.

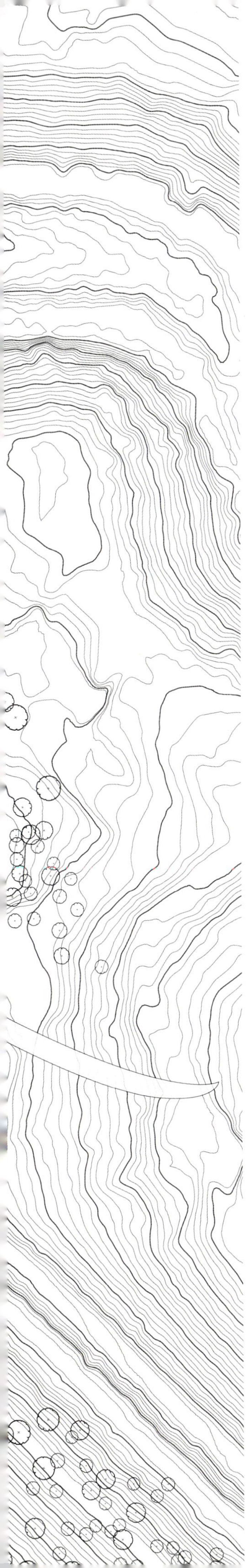

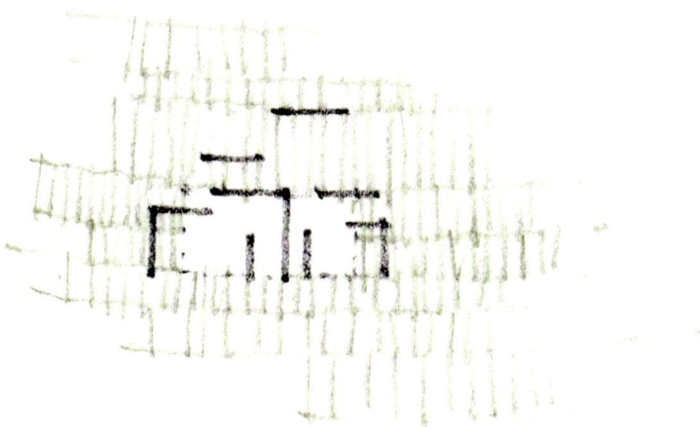

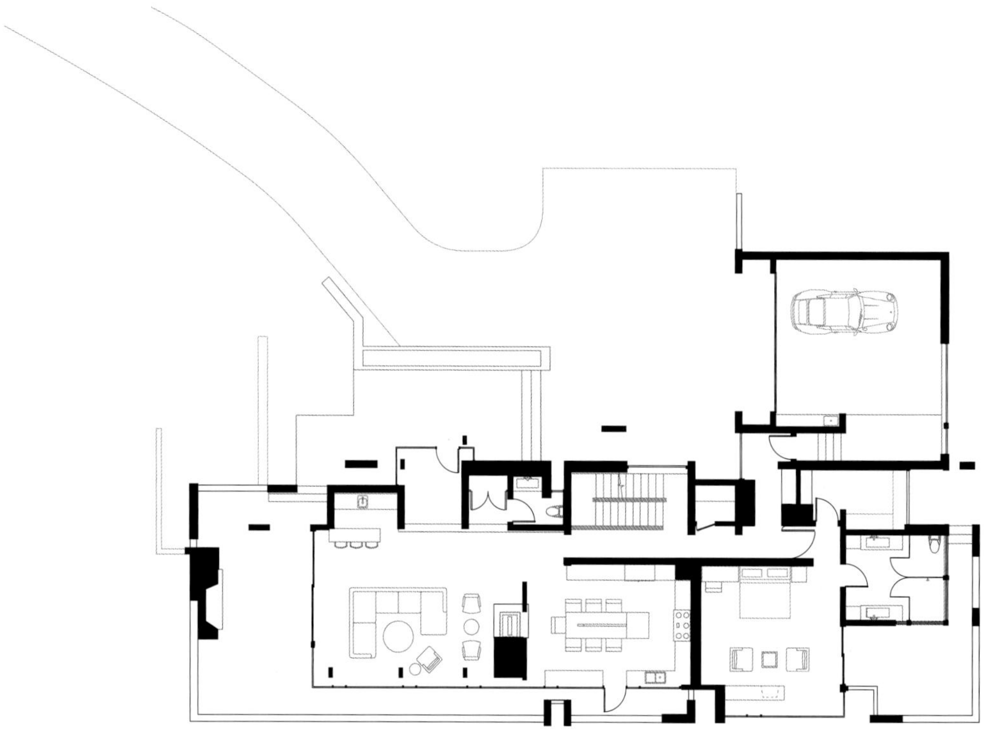

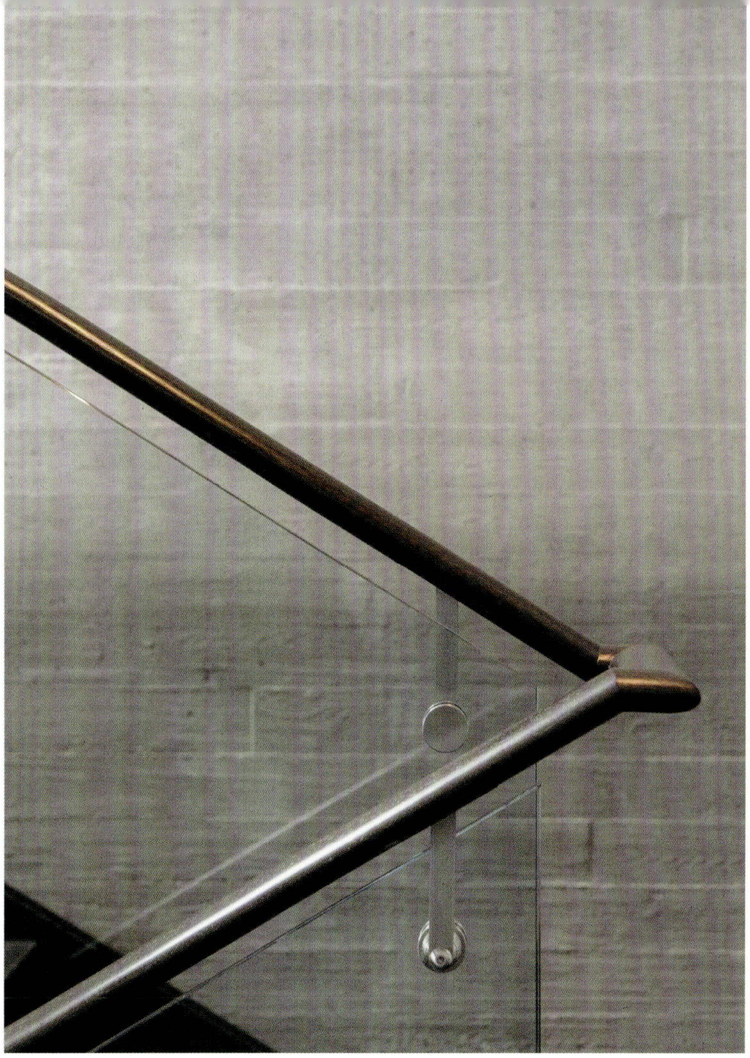

Opposite: Paired steel plates form the stair stringers. Minimally detailed, the glass handrail slips between the structural members, keeping the overall expression simple, strong, and open.

Top right: The stained wood handrail appears to float in space. Its ergonomic shape and slight texture are pleasing and surprising in the crisp composition.

Bottom right: Light and shadow animate the layered composition of concrete walls.

Gammel Damm

05 14

Old Snowmass, Colorado
11.76 Acres
Morgedal, Norway Cabin
Lichen Rock
6 Trees
Along the Land
Inside the Oaks
All or Some
Sauna for 10
4,320 Square Feet
Axes and Wood Chopping
Separate and Whole

09 01

Gammel Damm is a modern family retreat inspired by the client's rugged, multigenerational cabin located near Morgedal, Norway.

To provide privacy, the house is located at the interior of the site among several large spruce trees, scattered aspen groves, and scrub oaks; native sage is abundant on the gently sloping site. The owners wished to preserve the existing vegetation and restore the natural landscape directly adjacent to the house so they might live immersed in nature, absent lawns or other introduced landscaping.

By pulling apart individual program elements, separate building components are allowed to adapt to the sloping topography and minimize site disturbance. Unifying these elements is a singular sloped roof that parallels the natural grade and reinforces the building's relationship to the land. The landscape flows beneath the roof and between building elements, creating covered outdoor spaces and framing views to nature. At these locations, interior spaces extend into the landscape, layering together the experience of site and architecture.

Vertical weathered wood siding on the outer building skin shifts to black siding as the building forms recede under the sloping roof, giving the house a sculptural quality. Echoing the larger architectural moves, the vertical board siding is pulled apart, allowing filtered light into specific interior spaces. Natural materials continue to transition on the home's interior, becoming tone-on-tone oak expressed through individual boards as wall cladding and as vertical grain veneer millwork and built-in furniture. A granite fireplace anchors the interior and exterior living spaces and integrates with the continuous concrete floors that flow throughout the project.

In a final homage to the family's Norwegian cabin and the traditions built there, a "destination sauna" rests at the upper end of the compound, accessed via a covered boulder and stone pathway. Like the house to which it belongs, it defers to its surroundings at every turn.

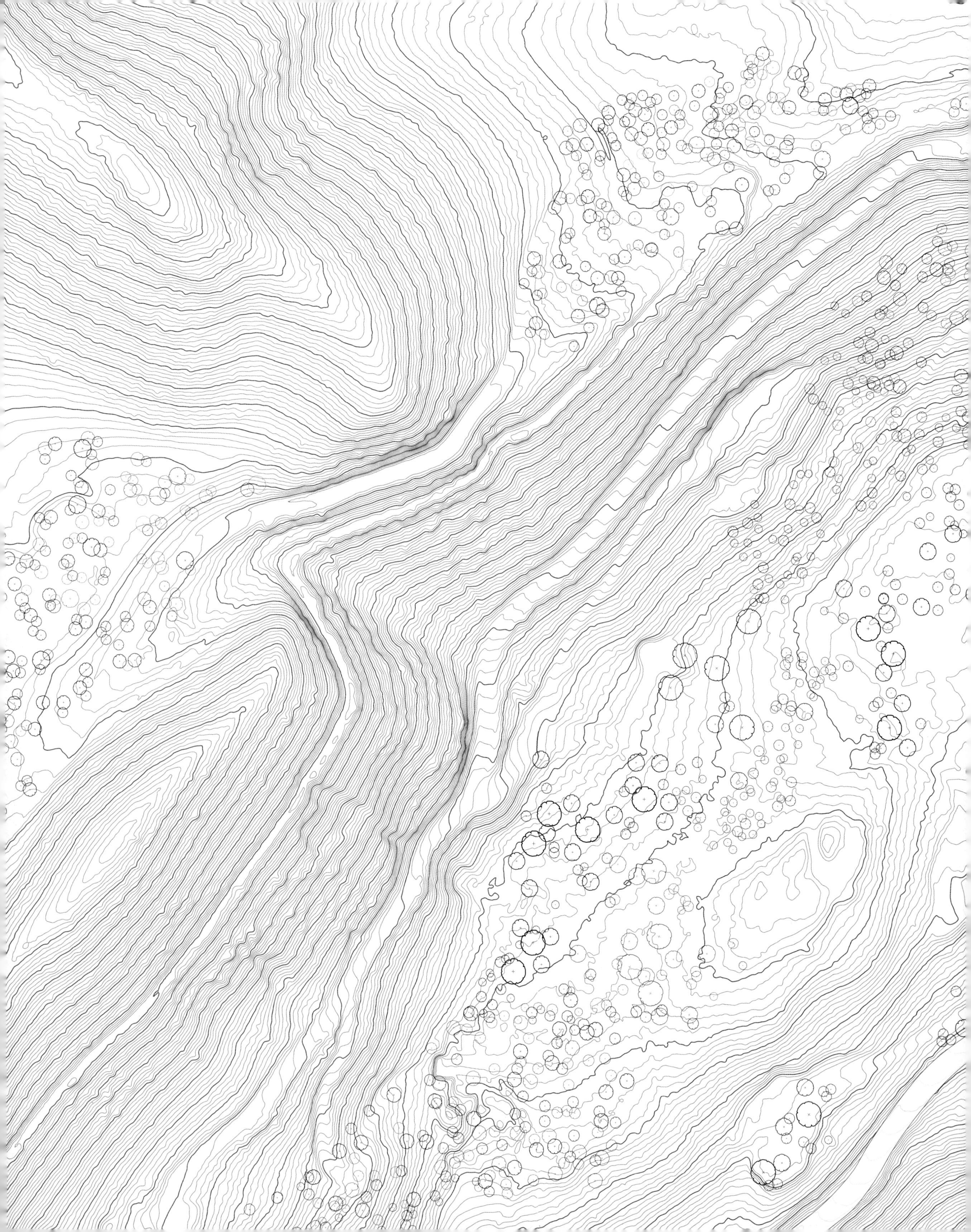

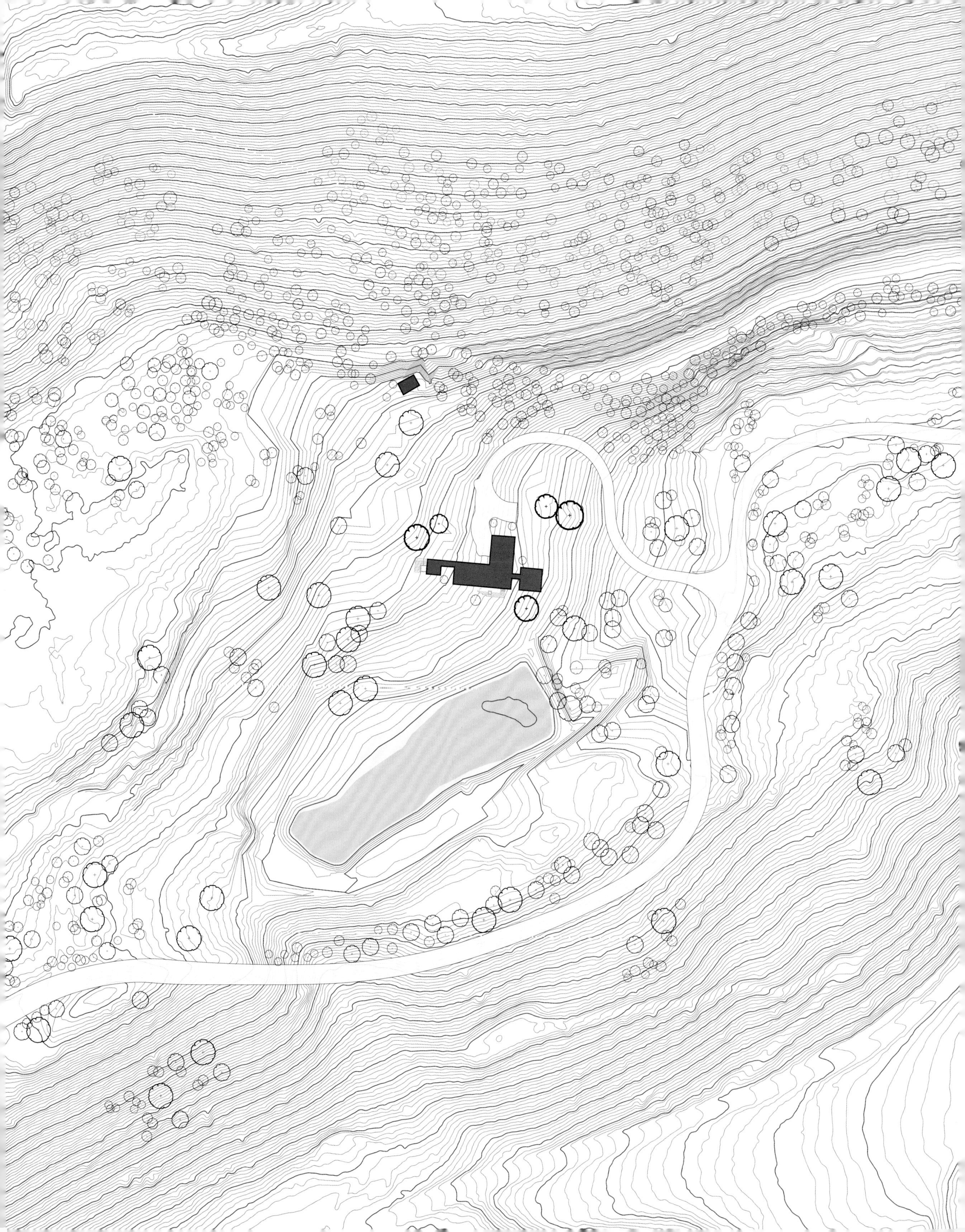

Opposite: A detail of the integrated sliding steel-and-glass door that spans the full width of the fireplace and stacked wood openings.

Above: The custom candle chandelier is a nod to the owners' Nordic roots. The subtle angle of the top mimics the roof slope in section.

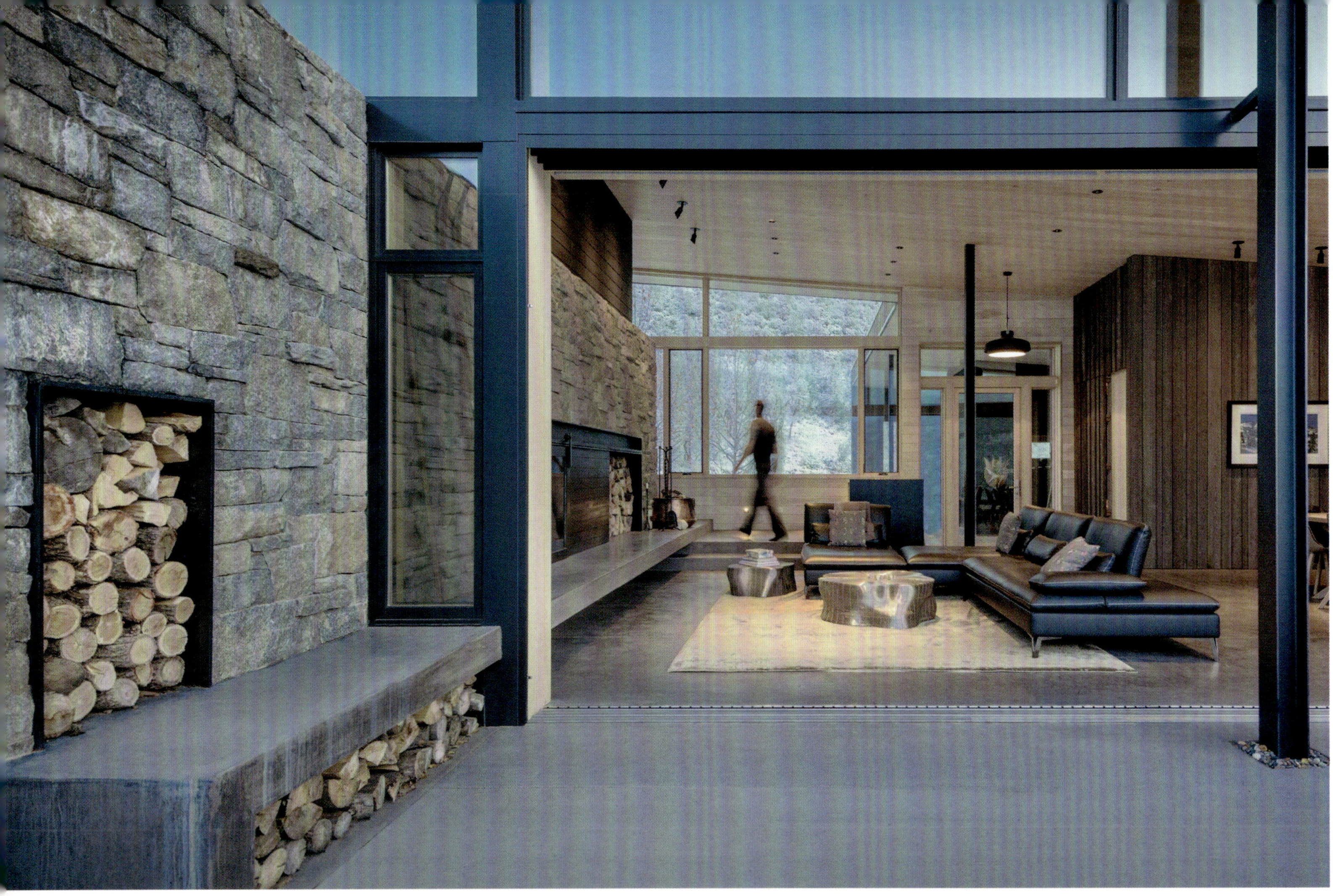

Top opposite: The fireplace and hearth stretch through the house and extend to the exterior.

Bottom opposite: The entry is defined by an integrated bench and storage piece. Just beyond, the mudroom can be concealed with a sliding door with vertical siding that aligns whether open or closed.

Top right: The concrete steps initiate the path to the sauna, transitioning to rustic stepping-stones on the exterior.

Bottom right: Monolithic steps are integrated with the hearth and allow adjacent rooms to adapt to the sloping topography.

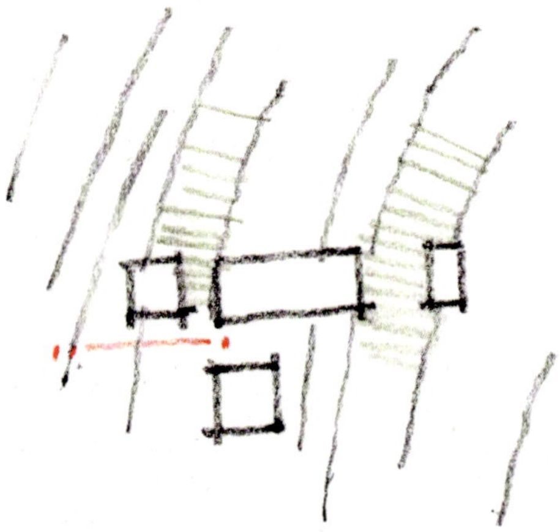

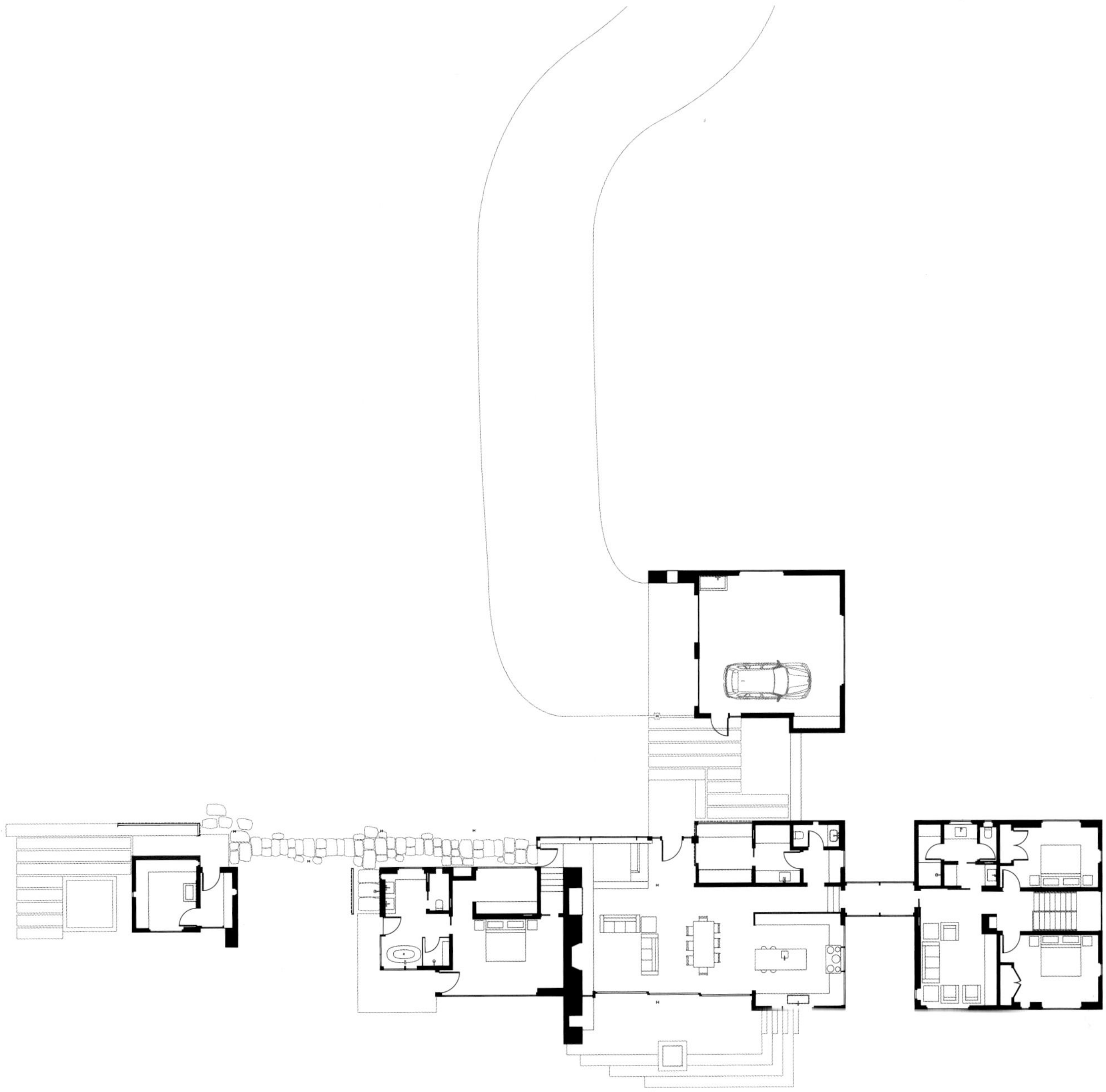

1989

Kanozan International Design Competition, Chiba Prefecture, Japan. Invitational competition, Bronze Award.

The Little Nell opens, one of the earliest boutique hotels in a resort setting.

Hagman Yaw Architects is the AIA Colorado and Western Mountain Region Firm of the Year.

Wolves are reintroduced into Yellowstone National Park.

1995

1998

Wise Residence recognized in the Chicago Athenaeum's American Architecture Awards.

Cottle Graybeal Yaw opens world headquarters in Basalt—and celebrates its 27th annual ski day.

1999

2000

Aspen Mountain's Sundeck Restaurant, the first LEED Certified building in a resort.

The Aspen Skiing Company is one great client—industry leaders, sustainable pioneers, great values, smart.

Architecture of the New West, CGY's first monograph.

2001

2004

Design begins on Red Mountain Residence. Bold concrete forms put it on the map in the old mining town.

1949

The worldwide Goethe Bicentennial is held in Aspen, Colorado. It leads to the formation of the Aspen Music School, the International Design Conference in Aspen, and the Aspen Institute. This synergy of body, mind, and spirit becomes known as the Aspen Idea, and fuels a creative community.

Four hippies form Copeland Finholm Hagman Yaw Architects.

1971

1972

"Rocky Mountain High" is released.

Copland Finholm Hagman Yaw Architects design John Denver's house.

The Aspen Airport opens, the largest passively heated building in the United States.

1976

Copeland Hagman Yaw's United States Post Office prototype, with passive and active solar systems, opens in Aspen.

1978

1980

Yaw Residence is featured in *Record Houses*

Steve Jobs presents the concept for the personal computer at the International Design Conference in Aspen.

Environmental Protection Act is created.

1983

1987

The Inn at Semiahmoo in Blaine, Washington. Hagman Yaw's first major project completed outside of Colorado.

Notable History

If past is indeed prologue, the energy and passion in the firm today has solid foundations. A few noteworthy events in the firm's past give us reason to look forward with great anticipation.

Acknowledgments

Sharing our work and approach through this book is an opportunity to reflect and thank those who have contributed to it.

First and foremost, our clients have humbled us with their energy, intellect, vision, and values. It has been one of the gifts of our careers to work with so many inspiring people. We hope that sharing our love for design has been as enriching for you as sharing your lives has been for us. Our deepest appreciation.

Collaboration is an overused term but completely integral to our studio. Starting with Larry Yaw, who set the tone for serious work and having a good time doing it, we have fed off of the collective passions of the architects and designers who have made our studio a place where laughter, opinions, and enthusiasm have never been in short supply. Thank you for your dedication and talent, for making the days more enjoyable and the work better.

Our work is hands-on, from reading a site to shaping spaces to bringing materials together. We have been so fortunate to work with some of the best landscape architects, builders, artisans, and designers any architect could hope for. They have challenged us and exceeded what could be reasonably expected, and we thank them for their inspired work.

This book couldn't have happened without the guidance and talent of Julie Kolar of Esse Design, who led us with her sophisticated graphic design sensibilities and so much more; Susan Cottle for clear editing advice; and our in-house team of Nicole Kinsler, Gage Reese, and Jenny Trumble, whose invaluable opinions, expertise, and wisdom have been freely given, even with their ever-pressing day jobs. For the final push we owe a tremendous debt of gratitude to Alan Rapp at Monacelli.

To our families who have supported our imperfect, never-ending efforts to balance deadlines, the pursuit of better design, and family life: thank you. We could not have done it without your understanding and encouragement.

John Cottle, Rich Carr, Alex Klumb, and Todd Kennedy

Eric Aanonsen
Susan Abel
Melanie Adkins
Malinda Allison
Ben Anderson
Erik Anderson
Colleen Avery
John Backman
Evan Barrett
Theresa Battle
Katie Bauer
Robert Baumen
Patrick Beaton
Philip Beck
James Benjamin
Hans Berglund
Rory Bilocerkowycz
Tracey Black
George Blume
Madelyn Blumenthal
Sue Bonet
Annatje Borchelt
Sarahliz Braugh
Colin Brice
Kenneth Bridges
Claire Britt
Barbara Britz
Stuart Brummett
Becky Brunson
Kevin Bukowski
Brandon Burns
Jeff Busby
Michael Carpenter

Jennifer Carr
Adam Casias
Nicholas Chan
Cowan Chang
Huey-Ru Chang
Anastasia Chmel
Scott Christensen
Monique Coe
Jim Copland
Rebecca Cote
Barbara Courtney
Jessica Coyle
Tia Crocker
Lorie D'Alessio
Renee Dake
David Damon
Ann Darby
Brian Delaney
Kim Doose
Michael Doyle
Shannon Doyle
Laura Dwyer
Russell Dykann
Rose Eberli
Charlie Eckart
Simon Elliot
Andy Evans
Thomas Fagan
Daniel Ferguson
David Finholm
Nicki Finholm
Maggie Fitzgerald
Cody Gabaldon

Barry Gereb
Stephanie Gerwin
Megan Gill
Brian Golden
Erica Golden
Daniel Goldstein
Laura Grafel
Stephanie Grandjacques
Melanie Grant
Bruce Gray
Doug Graybeal
Gretchen Greenwood
Alex Griffin
David Gull
Tim Hagman
Mike Hamberg
Nils Hammerbeck
Mark Hardeman
Jim Hardy
Kellie Hassinger
Taylor Hayda
Cherie Haynes
Kara Heer
Debbie Hembel
Kristine Hengy
Mark Henthorn
Jerry Hobgood
Heidi Hoffman
Wren Hoffman
Mary Holley
Dale Hoover
John Houldin
Keith Howie

Christopher Jahn
Jayne Jensen
Oli Johansson
Dylan Johns
Karen Johnson
Merrill Johnson
Martin Jones
Tim Kieffer
Meredith Kielman
Michelle Kiese
Susie Kincade
Nicole Kinsler
Jeff Klein
Beth Knudson
Kip Kummer
Brian Kwekel
Lisa LaGuardia
Lauren Lahr
Emily Lawson
Matt Lee
Rye Lemons
Janet Leverson
Erik Lind
Jerry Logan
Jorah Lucca
Debra Lujan
Holly MacDonald
Bill Maron
Katie Marquette
Merfield Mata
Michael McCallister
Kerry McCarthy
Jeff McCollum

Past & Present

Scott McHale
Carrie McIntyre
Eileen McIntyre
Cat McMenimen
Nick Miscione
Caleb Mulvena
Jenny Narrod
Jordan Neal
David Needleman
Bjorn Nelson
Delvon Nemecheck
Joe Neys
Susan Nicholson
Alexander Nieuwland-Zlotnicki
Galen Nourjian
Sarah Nyman
Sean O'Bryant
Jamie Olson
Jennifer Olson
Rys Olson
Gail Orrick
Brian Paddack
Kyle Page
Asher Paxton
Melinda Pearson
Deborah Pease
Charles Pederson
Karen Peterson
Jim Petrie
Michelle Petruno
Jola Pieslak
Justin Ping
David Polich

Duncan Porteous
Fiona Porteous
Michael Pritchard
Michael Pukas
Matt Qual
Abelardo Ramirez Mon
Lori Rapaport
Kim Raymond
Graham Reed
Gage Reese
Anna Reynoso
Jon Rice
Jordan Rich
Chris Ridings
Dave Ritchie
Charles Rosenberg
Les Rosenstein
Jerry Ross
Mark Rudolf
Christina Ruotolo
Rob Russell
Ethan Ryden
Will Saltonstall
Peter Sante
Sean Satterfield
Laura Schappert
John Schenck
Johnathan Schiller
Chrystl Schuster
Charles Schwab
Steven Scollo
Robert Sharp
B.J. Smith

Matthew Smith
Theresa Snyder
Jill Spaeh
Dana Stangeland
Wayne Stryker
Reggie Stump
Annabelle Su
Pam Sudmeier
Thamronkeat Supawit
Kevin Swanson
George Switzer
Peter Szczelina
Lydia Szewczyk
Lisa Teal
Karrie Tenley
Andrew Thompson
Michael Thompson
Anna Timroth
Susan Touchette
Matthew Tracy
Robert Trimble
Jenny Trumble
Maura Trumble
Doug Unfug
Do-Yong Um
Jason Upper
Sheri Vail
Brandon Venable
Jake Vickery
Megan Voiles
Danika Voorhees
Anne Wachsler
Darby Watt

David Webster
Ken Wells
Chad Weltzin
John Wheeler
Amanda Whiting
Brian Wilson
Steve Wilson
Kevin Wolf
Cortney Woller
Julie Woodruff
Karen Woods
Iroy Worgull
Jodie Wright
Haisheng Xu
Ron Yaw
Natalie York
Will Young

Principals:
Rich Carr
John Cottle
Todd Kennedy
Alex Klumb
Robin Schiller
Chris Touchette
Larry Yaw

Past: 1971-2019
Present: 2020

2007 TELLURIDE MAGAZINE | MODERN BY DESIGN | VISION HILL
2007 MOUNTAIN LIVING | RESPONSIBLE DEVELOPMENT AWARD | BRASADA RANCH RESORT
2007 COLORADO HOMES & LIFESTYLES | MOUNTAIN MAJESTY | RYAN RESIDENCE
2008 ASPEN HOME MAGAZINE | QUIET ON THE WESTERN FRONT | CHASE RESIDENCE
2008 SKI AREA MANAGEMENT | THE ULTIMATE TREEHOUSE | SNOWMASS BASE VILLAGE TREEHOUSE
2008 BUILDER | 2008 BUILDER'S CHOICE WINNERS | OBERMEYER PLACE
2008 ASPEN SOJOURNER | THE RIGHT MIX | OBERMEYER PLACE
2008 MOUNTAIN HOMESTYLES | OF THE EARTH | WEINGARTEN RESIDENCE
2008 FORBES LIFE MOUNTAIN TIME | GREEN MACHINES | FERGUSON & CHASE
2008 VAIL HOME MAGAZINE | MOUNTAIN CONTEMPORANEOUS | BRANDT RESIDENCE
2008 BRICK IN ARCHITECTURE, SILVER AWARD | OBERMEYER PLACE
2008 US GREEN BUILDING COUNCIL, LEED GOLD | BRASADA RANCH- THE RANCH HOUSE
2009 DENVER MAGAZINE | SOARING ON BUTTERFLY WINGS | CONRAD RESIDENCE
2009 ASPEN MAGAZINE | NEW MOUNTAIN LIVING | CARR RESIDENCE
2009 MOUNTAIN LIVING | BLURRED BOUNDARIES | CHASE RESIDENCE
2009 LUXE | CONNECTED TO NATURE | DYER RESIDENCE
2010 AIA COLORADO WEST CHAPTER, CITATION AWARD | MAGNIFICO RESIDENCE
2010 AIA COLORADO WEST CHAPTER, CITATION AWARD | WALL HOUSE
2010 COLORADO HOMES & LIFESTYLES | MODERN LIFE | CARR RESIDENCE
2010 LUXE — COLORADO | UNEXPECTED DISCOVERY | LIPMAN RESIDENCE
2010 LUXE — NATIONAL | UNEXPECTED DISCOVERY | LIPMAN RESIDENCE
2011 AIA COLORADO, CITATION AWARD | MAGNIFICO RESIDENCE
2011 BUILDER'S CHOICE AWARDS, AWARD OF MERIT | LIMELIGHT LODGE
2011 SHELTER MAGAZINE | CLEAN LINES, VOLUPTUOUS VIEWS | THE PERFECT ARCHITECT
2011 COLORADO HOMES & LIFESTYLES | COME ON IN | SMITHBURG RESIDENCE
2011 WESTERN ART & ARCHITECTURE | INSPIRED PLACEMAKERS | CCY FIRM PROFILE
2011 ASPEN MAGAZINE | AN ARCHITECT'S HOME | COTTLE RESIDENCE
2011 LUXE — COLORADO | NATURE'S WAY | PRIVATE RESIDENCE
2012 AIA COLORADO, CITATION AWARD | WALL HOUSE
2012 BUILDER | MODERN FACE, OLD SOUL | COTTLE RESIDENCE
2012 ASPEN MAGAZINE | FRIENDS AND NEIGHBORS | MOUNTAIN VIEW RESIDENCE
2012 THE WALL STREET JOURNAL | THE NEW ANTI SKI HOUSE | CARR RESIDENCE
2013 COWBOYS & INDIANS | DISCOVER BRASADA RANCH | BRASADA RANCH
2013 LUXE — COLORADO | HOUSE BLEND | FILLER RESIDENCE
2013 SKI MAGAZINE | MOST INNOVATIVE DAY LODGE | ELK CAMP LODGE, SNOWMASS SKI AREA
2014 AIA COLORADO, AWARD OF MERIT, ARCHITECTURE | THE BRIDGE HOUSE
2014 AIA COLORADO WEST CHAPTER, AWARD OF MERIT | THE BRIDGE HOUSE
2014 AIA COLORADO WEST CHAPTER, AWARD OF MERIT | THE SNOWMASS TREEHOUSE RESIDENCE
2014 GOLD NUGGET AWARDS, INTERNATIONAL AWARD OF MERIT | CHANGCHUN DEER VALLEY RESORT
2014 LUXE GOLD LIST TOP 100 ARCHITECTS OF THE YEAR
2014 ASPEN MAGAZINE | INTERIORS COLORADO COVER | TIERNEY RESIDENCE
2014 ASPEN MAGAZINE | MODERN FAMILY | TIERNEY RESIDENCE
2014 ASPEN MAGAZINE | INTERIORS COLORADO | WEST END RESIDENCE
2014 ARCHITECTURAL RECORD | WOVEN INTO PLACE | ASPEN ART MUSEUM
2014 ASPEN MAGAZINE | BEYOND THE BEACH | THE FOOD AND WINE ISSUE
2014 ASPEN MAGAZINE | OUTSIDE IN | WEST END RESIDENCE
2014 THE DESIGN BUREAU 100 | TEN EASY WAYS TO INCORPORATE SUSTAINABLE DESIGN IN YOUR WORK | BY JOHN COT
2014 THE DESIGN BUREAU 100 | CONTEMPORARY COLORADO | STARWOOD RESIDENCE
2014 LUXE — COLORADO | NATURAL ALIGNMENT | SILVERMAN RESIDENCE
2015 AIA COLORADO | FIRM OF THE YEAR
2015 TOP MOUNTAIN ARCHITECTS 2015 | MOUNTAIN LIVING MAGAZINE
2015 OUTSIDE MAGAZINE BEST PLACES TO WORK | CCY ARCHITECTS
2015 US GREEN BUILDING COUNCIL, LEED Silver | SNOWMASS ELK CAMP RESTAURANT
2015 US GREEN BUILDING COUNCIL, LEED Gold | GAMBEL OAKS RANCH
2015 AIA WESTERN MOUNTAIN REGION, HONOR AWARD | ASPEN ART MUSEUM (ARCHITECT OF RECORD)
2015 AIA COLORADO, AWARD OF MERIT | ASPEN ART MUSEUM (ARCHITECT OF RECORD)
2015 AIA COLORADO WEST, MERIT AWARD | CASTLE CREEK RESIDENCE
2015 AIA COLORADO WEST, CITATION AWARD | OLD POND RESIDENCE
2015 AIA COLORADO WEST, CITATION AWARD | GAMBLE OAKS RANCH
2015 GOLD NUGGET AWARDS, AWARD OF MERIT | BUTTERMILK HIDEOUT
2015 GOLD LIST ARCHITECTS | LUXE COLORADO
2015 ASPEN MAGAZINE | EAST MEETS WEST | WOODY CREEK RESIDENCE
2015 ASPEN PEAK | SUSTAINABLE PROPERTIES DEFINE | CCY ARCHITECTS
2015 OUTSIDE MAGAZINE | TOP 100 BEST PLACES TO WORK IN THE U.S.
2015 LUXE - COLORADO | GOLD LIST ARCHITECTS | CCY ARCHITECTS
2016 AIA PECONIC CHAPTER DANIEL J. ROWEN MEMORIAL DESIGN AWARDS | MERIT AWARD UNBUILT PROJ
AIA COLORADO, AWARD OF EXCELLENCE | GAMBEL OAKS RANCH

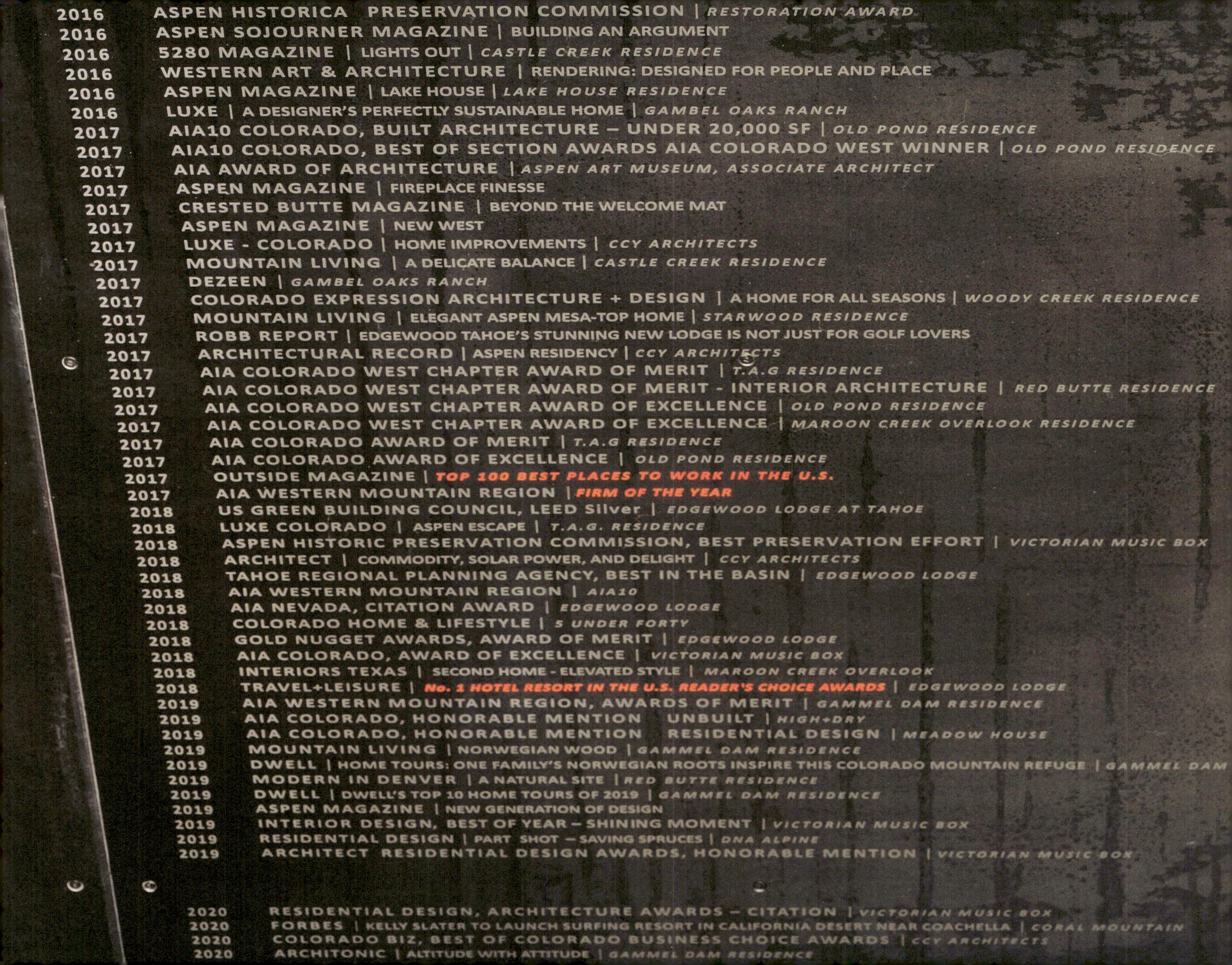
2016 ASPEN HISTORICA PRESERVATION COMMISSION | RESTORATION AWARD
2016 ASPEN SOJOURNER MAGAZINE | BUILDING AN ARGUMENT
2016 5280 MAGAZINE | LIGHTS OUT | CASTLE CREEK RESIDENCE
2016 WESTERN ART & ARCHITECTURE | RENDERING: DESIGNED FOR PEOPLE AND PLACE
2016 ASPEN MAGAZINE | LAKE HOUSE | LAKE HOUSE RESIDENCE
2016 LUXE | A DESIGNER'S PERFECTLY SUSTAINABLE HOME | GAMBEL OAKS RANCH
2017 AIA10 COLORADO, BUILT ARCHITECTURE – UNDER 20,000 SF | OLD POND RESIDENCE
2017 AIA10 COLORADO, BEST OF SECTION AWARDS AIA COLORADO WEST WINNER | OLD POND RESIDENCE
2017 AIA AWARD OF ARCHITECTURE | ASPEN ART MUSEUM, ASSOCIATE ARCHITECT
2017 ASPEN MAGAZINE | FIREPLACE FINESSE
2017 CRESTED BUTTE MAGAZINE | BEYOND THE WELCOME MAT
2017 ASPEN MAGAZINE | NEW WEST
2017 LUXE - COLORADO | HOME IMPROVEMENTS | CCY ARCHITECTS
2017 MOUNTAIN LIVING | A DELICATE BALANCE | CASTLE CREEK RESIDENCE
2017 DEZEEN | GAMBEL OAKS RANCH
2017 COLORADO EXPRESSION ARCHITECTURE + DESIGN | A HOME FOR ALL SEASONS | WOODY CREEK RESIDENCE
2017 MOUNTAIN LIVING | ELEGANT ASPEN MESA-TOP HOME | STARWOOD RESIDENCE
2017 ROBB REPORT | EDGEWOOD TAHOE'S STUNNING NEW LODGE IS NOT JUST FOR GOLF LOVERS
2017 ARCHITECTURAL RECORD | ASPEN RESIDENCY | CCY ARCHITECTS
2017 AIA COLORADO WEST CHAPTER AWARD OF MERIT | T.A.G RESIDENCE
2017 AIA COLORADO WEST CHAPTER AWARD OF MERIT - INTERIOR ARCHITECTURE | RED BUTTE RESIDENCE
2017 AIA COLORADO WEST CHAPTER AWARD OF EXCELLENCE | OLD POND RESIDENCE
2017 AIA COLORADO WEST CHAPTER AWARD OF EXCELLENCE | MAROON CREEK OVERLOOK RESIDENCE
2017 AIA COLORADO AWARD OF MERIT | T.A.G RESIDENCE
2017 AIA COLORADO AWARD OF EXCELLENCE | OLD POND RESIDENCE
2017 OUTSIDE MAGAZINE | TOP 100 BEST PLACES TO WORK IN THE U.S.
2017 AIA WESTERN MOUNTAIN REGION | FIRM OF THE YEAR
2018 US GREEN BUILDING COUNCIL, LEED Silver | EDGEWOOD LODGE AT TAHOE
2018 LUXE COLORADO | ASPEN ESCAPE | T.A.G. RESIDENCE
2018 ASPEN HISTORIC PRESERVATION COMMISSION, BEST PRESERVATION EFFORT | VICTORIAN MUSIC BOX
2018 ARCHITECT | COMMODITY, SOLAR POWER, AND DELIGHT | CCY ARCHITECTS
2018 TAHOE REGIONAL PLANNING AGENCY, BEST IN THE BASIN | EDGEWOOD LODGE
2018 AIA WESTERN MOUNTAIN REGION | AIA10
2018 AIA NEVADA, CITATION AWARD | EDGEWOOD LODGE
2018 COLORADO HOME & LIFESTYLE | 5 UNDER FORTY
2018 GOLD NUGGET AWARDS, AWARD OF MERIT | EDGEWOOD LODGE
2018 AIA COLORADO, AWARD OF EXCELLENCE | VICTORIAN MUSIC BOX
2018 INTERIORS TEXAS | SECOND HOME - ELEVATED STYLE | MAROON CREEK OVERLOOK
2018 TRAVEL+LEISURE | No. 1 HOTEL RESORT IN THE U.S. READER'S CHOICE AWARDS | EDGEWOOD LODGE
2019 AIA WESTERN MOUNTAIN REGION, AWARDS OF MERIT | GAMMEL DAM RESIDENCE
2019 AIA COLORADO, HONORABLE MENTION UNBUILT | HIGH+DRY
2019 AIA COLORADO, HONORABLE MENTION RESIDENTIAL DESIGN | MEADOW HOUSE
2019 MOUNTAIN LIVING | NORWEGIAN WOOD | GAMMEL DAM RESIDENCE
2019 DWELL | HOME TOURS: ONE FAMILY'S NORWEGIAN ROOTS INSPIRE THIS COLORADO MOUNTAIN REFUGE | GAMMEL DAM
2019 MODERN IN DENVER | A NATURAL SITE | RED BUTTE RESIDENCE
2019 DWELL | DWELL'S TOP 10 HOME TOURS OF 2019 | GAMMEL DAM RESIDENCE
2019 ASPEN MAGAZINE | NEW GENERATION OF DESIGN
2019 INTERIOR DESIGN, BEST OF YEAR – SHINING MOMENT | VICTORIAN MUSIC BOX
2019 RESIDENTIAL DESIGN | PART SHOT – SAVING SPRUCES | DNA ALPINE
2019 ARCHITECT RESIDENTIAL DESIGN AWARDS, HONORABLE MENTION | VICTORIAN MUSIC BOX
2020 RESIDENTIAL DESIGN, ARCHITECTURE AWARDS – CITATION | VICTORIAN MUSIC BOX
2020 FORBES | KELLY SLATER TO LAUNCH SURFING RESORT IN CALIFORNIA DESERT NEAR COACHELLA | CORAL MOUNTAIN
2020 COLORADO BIZ, BEST OF COLORADO BUSINESS CHOICE AWARDS | CCY ARCHITECTS
2020 ARCHITONIC | ALTITUDE WITH ATTITUDE | GAMMEL DAM RESIDENCE

Photography Credits

Tommy Andersson/ EyeEm via *Getty Images*
Uncovering 120

Aspen Historical Society, Aspen Times Collection John Denver singing at the Deaf Camp picnic, in the Aspen Times, June 17, 1976
Notable History 299

Aspen Skiing Company
Notable History 299

Ferenc Berko, courtesy BERKO Photo; Arthur Rubinstein, 1949
Notable History 299

Jeremy Bittermann
Uncovering 116; Meadow 130–135, 139, 140, 142–148, 150; Notes 294

JC Buck
T.A.G. 62, 64, 67, 69–75, 78-85

Center for Snow and Avalanche Studies
Uncovering 120

Jason Dewey
Red Mountain 256

Mimi Ditchie Photography/Moment via *Getty Images*
Notes 290

Eyecrave/E+ via *Getty Images*
Introduction 08

Raul Garcia | Astula
Castle Creek 18, 20, 22, 25, 26, 30–37; Bridge 193–197, 200, 202, 204, 206, 211–213

Art Gray
Gambel Oaks Ranch 88, 92, 97–101, 103–105, 108, 110

Dennis Hlynsky, *Fruit Flies Describe a Bowl of Fruit*
Connecting 184

Nick Johnson
Bridge 203, 208

Kissane Viola Design kissaneviola.com
Notable History 299

Kjschoen/E+ via *Getty Images*
Table of Contents 10

Patrick Lienen/Moment via *Getty Images*
Introduction 05

Alan Majchrowicz/ Photodisc via *Getty Images*
Notes 289

David Marlow
Uncovering 122; Castle Creek 17, 28, 35; Maroon Creek Overlook 216, 219, 221, 226, 230–235; Red Mountain 238–240, 257–258; Notable History 299

Robert Millman
Uncovering 123; Notable History 299

Michael Moran
Notable History 299

Ralph Morse/The LIFE Images Collection via *Getty Images*
Notable History 299

Lena Nicholson
Introduction 01, 07; Foreword 12; Victorian Music Box 42, 55, 56; T.A.G. 61, 76, 78; Meadow House 137, 145; Maroon Creek Overlook 215, 224, 228, 229

Shawn O'Connor
Notable History 299

David Patterson
Gambel Oaks Ranch 90, 95, 106, 107

David Rumsey Map Collection, David Rumsey Map Center, Stanford Libraries
Uncovering 119

Helen H. Richardson/ *Denver Post* via *Getty Images*
Uncovering 118

Lindsey Ross, *Self Portrait*
Connecting 182

Jeremy Swanson
Notable History 299

Ron and Patty Thomas/ E+ via *Getty Images*
Notes 292

USDA Forest Service, Geospatial Service and Technology Center (GSTC)
Uncovering 119

USGS Department of the Interior
Uncovering 119

Brandon Venable
Uncovering 120

Westend61 via *Getty Images*
Uncovering 118

Draper White
Introduction 04, 14; Uncovering 118, 122, 123, 124; Victorian Music Box 40, 44, 45, 47, 48, 50–53, 55, 56–59; Red Butte 153–159, 161, 164–175; Maroon Creek Overlook 224, 225; Red Mountain 237, 242, 243, 245, 248–251, 253–255; Gammel Damm 262–267, 269, 272–280, 282–287; Notes 296, 297; Notable History 308, 310

Larry Yaw
Red Mountain 241
Notable History 299

Library of Congress Control Number: 2020949993

ISBN 978-1-58093-577-7

10 9 8 7 6 5 4 3 2 1

Printed in China

Design by Julie Kolar, Esse Design
Edited by Susan Cottle
Additional contributions by John Cottle, Rich Carr, Todd Kennedy, Alex Klumb, Gage Reese, Jenny Trumble, Nicole Kinsler

Monacelli
65 Bleecker Street
New York, New York 10012

www.monacellipress.com